OUT OF YOUR MIND

Eddie Shapiro was born in New York City in 1942 and as a teenager won the New York City dance championships. In 1968 he trained in India and became a monk. There he laid the foundation of the work that he and his wife, the well-known author **Debbie Shapiro**, have dedicated their lives to. Debbie was born in England in 1953 to a Quaker background. She trained for many years in bodymind therapy and in traditional Eastern meditation. Together they have received personal teachings from H.H. the Dalai Lama, H.E. Tai Situpa, and from prominent Indian Yogis.

The Shapiros are inspired workshop leaders who often present at international conferences, have appeared on television, radio and in many magazines. They live in Boulder, Colorado, where Eddie is a freestyle skier.

Eddie and Debbie Shapiro have been recognized by their peers as individuals who are making a major contribution to the uplifting of individual and social consciousness. Bernie Siegel, MD, author of bestselling *Love, Medicine and Miracles*, says, 'Eddie and Debbie Shapiro are two warm, capable and caring individuals. Their work makes our planet a safer and more loving place to be.'

GW00724731

Edited by Eddie and Debbie Shapiro

THE WAY AHEAD

Also by Eddie Shapiro

INNER CONSCIOUS RELAXATION

Also by Debbie Shapiro

THE BODYMIND WORKBOOK
THE HEALER'S HANDBOOK
THE METAMORPHIC TECHNIQUE

OUT OF
YOUR MIND –
THE ONLY PLACE TO BE!

Eddie and Debbie Shapiro

ELEMENT
Shaftesbury, Dorset ● Rockport, Massachusetts

© Eddie and Debbie Shapiro 1992

Published in Great Britain in 1992 by
Element Books Limited
Longmead, Shaftesbury, Dorset

Published in the USA in 1992 by
Element, Inc
42 Broadway, Rockport, MA 01966

Cover illustration by Martin Jordan
Cover design by Max Fairbrother
Designed by Roger Lightfoot
Illustrations by Anne Ward
Typeset by Colset Pte Ltd.
Printed and bound in Great Britain by
Billings Ltd, Hylton Road, Worcester

British Library Cataloguing Data available

Library of Congress Cataloging Data available

ISBN 1-85230-306-9

Dedicated to all our teachers who have helped us to get out of our minds, including the late Harry and Edna Shapiro.

Contents

1

Being in Your Mind is like Being in a Paper Bag

Sarah is a beautiful woman – tall, blond and a gifted classical musician. However, despite her attributes, she was in therapy for three years suffering from low self-esteem and a lack of confidence. She felt trapped in her mind, unable to get free of the constant worries and fears that so plagued her. After three years she had stopped the therapy feeling she was at a dead end having hit an invisible wall that she could not penetrate. Sarah felt like a hopeless failure and that she would never succeed in resolving the mental chatter in her head.

A year later we met Sarah at one of our workshops. The breakthrough came for her when, with tears rolling down her face, she discovered that she did not have to try to find the answers in her mind. Instead she could enter into the loving and self-nurturing energy of her heart. Sarah saw how she had been trapped in her head as if she was in a paper bag, trying to resolve her issues yet unable to see beyond them.

Have you ever wondered how extraordinary the mind is? How it can reach from the sublime heights of intellectual ecstasy to the depths of suicidal despair, from piercing clarity to confused schizophrenia? It is the same mind that longs for that sumptuous creamy dessert or that stunning dress or suit, then afterwards wonders why we ate something so rich, or lets the clothing go unworn in the closet and feels guilty that we bought it in the first place!

This mind is capable of understanding the most intricate scientific and mathematical theories and can make complicated corporate decisions, yet the same mind can get caught up in trivia and nonsense, becoming upset or even unglued over a seemingly harmless remark. It runs our lives, pushing and pulling us in all directions, from attraction to repulsion, creating endless dramas, acting out our insecurities and fears.

It is this aspect of the mind that is most fascinating: the part of us that can go from being a genius one minute to being a basket case the next! There is no denying the importance and value of the mind – there is great brilliance and beauty inherent within the mind itself – but here we are looking at its more absurd and confused aspects. Thinking, for instance, is itself not wrong at all, but are our thoughts constructive ones or do they generate further confusion? For no matter how intellectually astute or creative we may be, this aptitude often has little or no effect upon the habitual mind and its repetitive patterns: the fear, guilt, suspicion, anxiety, neurosis, shame and lack of confidence.

These issues are buried inside the unconscious and seep through into our behaviour and relationships. A great deal of energy is used in attempting to ignore them! Greeting the world with a smile, with an 'Everything's fine, thank you', we

Being in Your Mind is like Being in a Paper Bag

immerse ourselves in mentally consuming activities or with endless domestic detail, so that eventually there is little time in which personal issues can be realistically dealt with. Perspective is lost and not enough attention is paid to that which is so debilitating in our lives. We become helpless, if not even frivolous and end up going to others – to professionals – to do the unravelling for us.

Hidden patterns of behaviour and unconscious motivations are always present and influencing us. Affected by our family and early life, our environment, friends and culture, these experiences then colour our reactions as we mature. In effect, we are the sum total of all that has gone before us, each event and experience influencing our development, particular beliefs, behavioural characteristics and attitudes. The traumas and conflicts of our lives are hidden in the unconscious. In becoming adults we are then confronted with the effect of these influences; they form the motivations that constantly influence our activities and feelings. Thus, falling out of a tree as a child may result in a fear of heights as an adult, or equally in a fear of being shouted at whenever we do something wrong.

For instance, if a girl experiences abuse or rejection by a male figure in her early life, then it is possible that she will look for that level of rejection in her relationships with men later on. When the rejection takes place it simply reaffirms the reality she knows as normal. It may hurt, it may be a painful reality, but it is the one with which she is familiar. In this situation it is almost impossible for her to accept love without waiting for, or making it turn into a rejection. Naturally no one would, in any logical or sane way, be looking for rejection or pain – that would be madness, for we all want to be loved and to be happy – but our habitual behaviour does one thing as our rational mind tells us another.

Alternatively, if a child experiences abuse then this incident may become buried so deeply that there is no conscious recollection of it. As Robert Bly says in *Iron John*, 'Denial stands for amnesia, forgetfulness, oblivion. An ocean of oblivion sweeps over a child when it is shamed. A woman is sexually abused at four and forgets the event entirely until she is thirty-eight . . . Denial means we have been entranced; we live for years in a trance.' As we mature problems can then arise in our ability to maintain relationships or with our sexuality. When this happens these past traumatic impressions may be uncovered. The effects of the oblivion will have to be dealt with as we become aware of the denial. If further abuse is experienced as an adult then we may find we are not just dealing with the present violation, but also with the buried feelings from past violations, all emerging at once.

So many contrary opinions are conditioned into our being – we are attacked and hurt, taught conflicting attitudes towards sex, towards our bodies, told that it is our duty to make money, to have children. An alcoholic father tells us it is wrong to drink; or we get caught between parents who, in a warring divorce, say they only want the best for us. Most of us have a story, one of abuse or neglect, rejection, hurt, misunderstanding, anger or suppression, and these become compounded over the years.

Recognizing the Patterns

However, it is easy to blame the past without taking the time to look a little more closely. For the issues we constantly seem to have to deal with in our lives, whether it be difficulties with money, with relationships and sexuality or with our health, are not always the real problem.

What is more often the difficulty is the fact that there is an inbuilt conditioned mental pattern of behaviour towards these issues; a pattern that has been deeply entrenched and maintained over the years. This may be an attitude of being a victim (I'm always being hurt; I always get sick at this time of year; I'll never be rich), or one of being a victor (no one can hurt me; no one can help me; I can look after myself). It is the mental pattern that is stuck, locked into a repetitive mode, regardless of the problem. For it makes no difference who we may be – from a housewife to a world leader – all are just as vulnerable and as easily influenced by the conditioned mind.

The strongest issue most of us have to deal with is the emphasis on 'winner takes all'. This is the idea that serving self first is more important than serving another. Such an attitude is based on the belief that we are all separate from each other: that I can win despite its meaning that you lose, that I can hurt you without hurting myself, that I can take more even though that leaves you with less. We are so caught up in ourselves and our needs that the effect we have on others becomes basically unimportant to us compared to seeking the rewards we want.

An abuser, for instance, is so immersed in his or her own pain and the urge to find release from that pain, that the effect of the abuse on the abused is often not consciously acknowledged. It is only when there is awareness of the essential connectedness between all beings that we see the effect of our actions. We then further realize that we are as intimately bound to that effect as the recipient is. Thus those who abuse or hurt others could actually be doing themselves more damage than they may be to the one they are abusing, for the pain and hurt that they are projecting on to the abused is the pain they are denying in themselves.

Few of us are free thinkers. Generally we are conditioned from early life to believe in labels: profession, country, religion. These labels are like credentials through which we identify ourselves. They form the content, that which gives meaning to our lives. We find our identity through our job, our spouse's job, our children, our illnesses, our hardships. Labels are used such as housewife, businessman, student, abuser, victim of abuse, recovering alcoholic, actress, healer, channel. The label stays as long as it is needed, as long as it serves us, for without our content there is a sense of having no identity.

This does not mean we have to be a victim of our patterns, are helpless and simply have to suffer our lot, for ultimately we are not the content – the true Self is essence which is always free. But it can mean tremendous commitment and motivation to go beyond such attitudes, to see through the conditioning, through the need for credentials. It calls for an honesty and self-awareness to be objective about our own behaviour: how we so easily become immersed in neurosis or act out past dramas.

The Chakras

The self-centred reality described above, where 'I' is the centre of the universe and 'other' is not acknowledged as important, is incorporated in the first and second of the *chakras*. The chakras are an integral part of the Eastern teachings, being found in both Yoga and Buddhism, as well as other esoteric traditions. The chakras – of which there are seven major ones – are often depicted as wheels or centres, but what they really imply are levels of being and ways of perceiving life. Each chakra represents a different level of consciousness, going from the gross or animal level to the subtle or divine.

The majority of humans function at the level of the first and second chakras. The first chakra deals with survival and fear, while the second deals with the conditioned mind, pleasure, pain and sensuality. Each one of us has the basic impetus firstly to survive and then to seek comfort.

The remaining five chakras become active as latent consciousness is awakened. Thus we develop our perception, moving from an unconscious level of awareness to the emergence of the superconscious. Each chakra denotes a further developmental state of conscious awareness and degree of understanding in a continually progressive movement – as perception awakens and we expand our awareness, then our realization of the nature of reality broadens and becomes more profound and clear. It is like a dance, an unfolding, or the opening of a flower.

Humankind has come a long way in terms of physical evolution; we have developed our world beyond any other known life form and have achieved enormous technical advancement, but collectively there is still a long way to go in the evolution of consciousness. *Evolution* takes us from the gross to the subtle, while *involution* takes us from the subtle to the sublime. We have yet to touch the depth of true wisdom and liberation that is our natural state by turning within instead of outside ourselves.

Understanding the chakra system helps to explain this conscious development that humankind experiences. It clarifies the difficulties, stresses and limitations that are encountered on the way and can deter us from realizing our full potential. Thus the difficulties experienced in life are in relationship to the level of consciousness of chakra we are functioning from. For instance, are we predominantly sensuous, based in our desires? Do we live primarily within the duality of pleasure and pain? Is power our main thrust in life? Or are we loving, compassionate and caring? Are we able to see beyond the limitations of the mind and experience inner peace?

The First Chakra

The essence of our survival instinct, fear and neurosis, is rooted in the energy of the first chakra and extends to the second chakra. This means that it is difficult to see beyond or through the influence of these energies, for here the consciousness is of a very primordial and self-centred nature.

We are generally unaware of our inner selves (other than in a simplistic way), of our behaviour, our neurotic and discursive mind. We tend to be unaware of such tendencies because the superficial is considered normal, that this is just how people are and what life is about. There is rarely the realization that we could be different. And it is not at all easy to rise above this unawareness for there is a tendency to cling to habitual patterns as a means of gaining security and safety. Without them we feel lost and unsure.

The first chakra indicates the struggle for survival. Traditionally this is known as the root chakra as the influence of this level of consciousness is at the root of all existence. Here lies the original source of life; from here all possibilities exist, all potential can be manifested. However, for potential to arise on a mundane level we first have to deal with survival.

Our preoccupation with survival nowadays has gone beyond just instinctual needs, to being preoccupied with neurotic and fearful survival. No longer directly foraging for food, we are instead constantly exposed to the threat of murder, rape, war and violence; pollution and environmental concerns are affecting our health; those living in the cities hide behind five locks on their doors and bars on their windows, then try to lose themselves in watching television; we are afraid to be alone or to walk in the dark; we live our lives as if someone will take it from us at any moment. Instead of seeing life as a treasure it is experienced as a great burden.

The stress created from this fear of survival is panic, anxiety, paranoia and self-centredness. It is a limited awareness, where we are locked into our own self and are largely unaware of others. Convinced the world is after us, we have to fight everyone and everything or it will get us first. Therefore we either hide and live in terror of attack, or become aggressive and violent. In the need to find some sort of identity and place in the world we surround ourselves with material objects, as if the very possessions themselves somehow create this longed-for sense of belonging.

This first chakra or level of consciousness represents our fear and hopelessness, our questions concerning the will to live or not. It incorporates all aspects of survival. But from survival comes the rising up of desire and the passion for life. This is the energy that can take us to the highest ecstasy – from the darkness and primal energies can arise supreme consciousness. So although the description of this chakra is of a basic, instinctive nature, it is also the starting point for the journey to higher understanding; it is the very mud from which can grow the lotus flower. In fact, we cannot proceed on the path of awakening without accepting and even embracing this level of our being.

In *Zen Mind, Beginner's Mind*, Shunryu Suzuki speaks of 'mind weeds' and how we should be grateful for our weeds because eventually they will become enriching. These weeds are all those thoughts and fears that congest and limit our movement forward, like the weeds in a pond that hinder the water from flowing. Evolution takes place when there is some understanding of how the weeds in our minds can become fertile food for self-nourishment and can feed our involution.

The Second Chakra

The second chakra, although indicative of consciousness that is still operating within the conditioned mind, begins to awaken the energy of desire on a mundane level. This is the realm of sensory pleasure and procreation – one way of ensuring survival is through creating the next generation!

However, if we have a suspicious or fearful nature then this energy can invoke sexual perversion, abuse and greed, rather than sharing and sensitivity. It also stimulates the desire to dominate or be dominated, to accumulate, to control or to be controlled. Too much stimulus of this chakra may cause an addiction to pleasurable experiences, regardless of their long-term effect. The consciousness functioning from this second chakra is therefore one of contrasts – of good and bad, up and down, light and dark. It operates within the realm of duality, of us and them, of you and me, of separation rather than unity.

The stress here is one of disappointment and unfulfilled longing, for pleasure on the mundane level never comes without pain. The world is a place of dualities and the more that sensory pleasure is sought, the more its opposite will dominate. However, the delusion is so strong that we believe one can be had without the other; thus most of our time is spent seeking the pleasurable and trying to avoid the painful! But the laws of the universe are in constant balance and it is inevitable that these two conditions go hand-in-hand. This inseparability of pleasure and pain then creates a resistance to change, for if change means pain then we will hold on as hard as we can to the pleasure we have!

In this way we become fixed, unable to be free or spontaneous. For spontaneity can imply a lack of control, powerlessness, or even vulnerability to attack from outside. Holding on and becoming fixed in our patterns and behaviour means that we can stay dominant, manipulating events exactly as we want them. This is often at the expense of other people's needs and wishes, such as with the abuser who has no regard for the feelings of the abused. The need to take control and fulfil our desire is greater than the awareness of the effect such desire has. In our search for an experience of pleasure we can therefore cause great suffering and misery.

Becoming sensitive and aware of others is one way of dealing with the energy of this consciousness: to replace desire with a contentment for what is; to accept change without fear. As we feel the pull of our desires or are immersed in fixed opinions and attitudes then this energy can be used to give instead of needing to get, to become flexible, to see the play of the opposites and to release their hold.

This second chakra also represents the unconscious, the collective unconscious that contains all the ancestral memory and built-in conditioning and understanding that mankind has accumulated. We have already mentioned how we learn to behave and react to life by the events that have happened over the years. But it is also true that contained within us is everything that mankind as a whole has ever experienced.

It is as if there is an aeroplane's black box built inside us, recording not only every experience we have ever had, but those that have happened to others throughout the ages as well. Everything is filed away, from where it subtly influences our behaviour and attitudes. This accumulated knowledge can be used to validate and reinforce our neurosis, or it can be used as a springboard towards deeper understanding. Are we trapped by our fears – a victim of our own self-centredness – or can we see through the insubstantiality of such issues to what is really meaningful?

Attempting Solidity

The limited consciousness of these first two chakras is due to the belief in ourselves as solid and fixed. The conviction that there is a real me is so powerful that we regard ourselves and our experiences very seriously. Yet every so often, beneath this self-created fixed image, we find the ominous suspicion that there is actually something very unsolid and insubstantial!

Many of us have such moments of awareness, a sneaky suspicion that all is not as we think it is, that in one way or another life is not so substantial and real after all. In fact, we all have an innate knowledge, intimate to our very being, that we are in reality groundless and impermanent, even fragile and tender. However, this knowledge, rather than being an inspiration to look further and find out what it really means, usually creates a fearful, desperate and desirous need to hold on tight so that the insubstantiality appears solid and our continuing existence therefore safe.

Namkhai Norbu says in *The Cycle of Day and Night*,

> The nature of the mind is like a highly polished mirror, whereas the individual thoughts, emotions, impulses, feelings, sensations, etc., which arise are like the reflections in this mirror . . . . With presence and awareness we live in the condition of the mirror, so to speak, whereas with ignorance we live in the condition of the reflections, thinking that whatever appears before us is substantial and real.

We are thus caught in an interesting paradox! Intuitively, deep inside, we know that everything is unreal, insubstantial, even somewhat meaningless, yet to enter into this knowledge is scary, ungrounded in normal reality. Rather than dealing with this paradox by fearlessly entering into the unknown, we create an enormous array of paraphernalia – all the content in our lives – to support a solid structure of meaning. Once done, we rarely move out of this structure, like mice in a cage going round and round. We have a more complicated cage perhaps, but it is just as fixed, purposefully created to perpetuate our beliefs.

The unknown is the big problem. For the unknown contains the one thing that constantly disputes our efforts to be solid and that is death. At some point we are going to die, to be leaving this physical realm, and we will certainly not be taking anything or anyone with us! Yet we go on accumulating things and people, and grow in our attachment to them, in order to appear as if there really is something solid here, until the reality of leaving is well hidden.

Enormous changes take place in the course of our lives and many of us may experience different kinds of death – the death of who we think we are, the death of life as we know it – but physical death is always at a distance. The fear of it permeates our world in numerous ways, from the medical maintenance of life for years beyond what would have been a natural death, to a deep paranoia of the unknown and what it may do to us. As Bernie Siegel says, we all know we are going to die, but we spend our lives denying it.

We prefer to ignore death – which lies in the future – by holding on to the past and all the things that have already been experienced. For these events may have been painful and difficult, traumatic or life-changing, but we got through them safely and are here to tell the story, death did not trip us up on the way! So the past becomes safe and is constantly referred to. The future is unsafe, for the future implies being different to how we are now, of being without that which maintains us, and few of us are willing to let go of such a carefully constructed support system! When things are going well then the future is bright and we look forward to it; but even then the thought of physical death can trigger resistance or panic.

This is very understandable, for physical death is the one thing that cannot be experienced until it happens. There is no one around who can explain it to us, no well-worn path or clear indication of what will occur. However, we may not voice our concerns as an actual fear of death, for that is simultaneously acknowledging that death exists. Rather it is expressed as a fear of change, of dealing with the unpredictable and therefore disconcerting and threatening aspects of life. This fear then becomes a sense of inadequacy, of not being able to cope, of being overwhelmed by the world. It may also manifest as restlessness, a twitching and nervousness – by keeping on the move we are able to avoid the reality staring us in the face.

The fear of physical death is a confrontation with impermanence. Ultimately, there is nothing in this world that is permanent, all things will die or dissolve at some time, whether it be our own lives, our relationships, health, or even our possessions, let alone the trees, animals and the world around us. Recognizing this fact and integrating its implications can actually be a very liberating experience for it frees us from the confines of having to control or hold on. We can let go and allow all things their rightful place in the universe. It is the recognition that if everything is in a constant state of change then there is no solidity, nothing fixed or identifiable, there is simply unfoldment. To be at peace with this is true freedom.

However, letting go of that to which we are attached is intricately connected to our ability to let go of our solidity, and this is where we stumble. It is far easier to let go of something we are not very attached to than it is to let go of that which supports the image of who we think we are! And so we suffer. The inability to accept the truth of transiency creates a longing for permanence, which can never be. As Shunryu Suzuki says, 'The teaching of the cause of suffering and the teaching that everything changes are thus two sides of the same coin.'

If our sense of solidity becomes insecure and uncertain we will seek out that which will support us. Yet there are no clear instructions to follow, nothing set up that is permanent and real. Moment by moment we have to deal with our own insubstantiality by ourselves. Trying to avoid this we enter into denial, blocking out those feelings that arise when confronted with impermanence. We build our fortifications and self-centredness to protect ourselves from this reality.

Being in a Paper Bag

The creation of these fears and neuroses is actually the creation of bars around our being, each bar representing a different neurosis that locks in the habitual patterns and behaviour. For freedom is too scary to consider – it involves too much change. As we get older these bars become like iron, immovable and fixed. How often we say, 'This is the way I am, this is me, it's too late for me to change now.' We identify with our thoughts and opinions as being real and justifiable – believing that it is impossible to change, therefore we just have to live with and suffer our imperfections.

But imagine you were free of all the limitations and difficulties you are dealing with, see if you can actually create that vision of being free of who you think you are! Just close your eyes and see yourself as a completely free being with nothing stopping you from being or doing anything you want to. You *can* be happy! You *can* be free!

As we do this visualization it is fascinating to find that our immediate response is invariably one of anxiety – it feels scary, there is an emptiness, a void, without the familarity we know. Even in our imagination freedom appears overwhelming because it is so unknown, so different. Despite our constrictions and limitations having such a debilitating effect, they are still preferable to the idea of being without them, for they are known whereas freedom is not.

So rather than enter into this emptiness, or confront the scariness and see what substantiality it actually has – if any – we hold on to the past, on to everything that has already happened, no matter how painful it was, and no matter how much pain it is still bringing. The pain of the past is preferable to the scary unknown. The pain is familiar, we are used to it. In fact it makes up the very fabric and substance of our lives because without it is the possibility that we do not exist. Pain provides the feeling of being real, of being someone or something. It becomes our identity and gives us a sense of solidity; it validates our ego and our unhappiness. Without it we would have to be happy!

Clinging to the pain suggests we are dragging this great sack of antiques around with us, this huge bag full of past memories and incidents. However, as we go along the sack bangs on the ground behind us so that all the antiques eventually get broken into small pieces. We have no complete memories left, only fragments, yet we even cling to these. This sack is carried everywhere we go and when the present reality gets too much to bear we pull out the appropriate reaction or issue and indulge in it as long as we need to. In so doing the past is kept alive and well. By acting as if the future were not there our fear of it cannot affect us.

Living in the mental plane of memories, intellectualization and analysis is living without being able to experience or even express real feeling and a deeper involvement with life. It is not nourishing or spiritually uplifting. There is no contact with the rhythms and impulses of life, with the seasons, the animals, the winds and the sun, or even with our own happiness. Instead these things are intrusions into our routine, they get in the way of our being able to function. For the mind becomes confined within itself, convoluted, engaging in numerous reasons for it to stay a certain way. In so doing it can perpetuate its own habitual patterns. In this discursive state the mind is unable to feel, to communicate or move freely, it eventually becomes stuck, even rigid.

Being in the mind is like being in a paper bag for there is no escape, no warmth of expression, it is claustrophobic. All that can be seen are our own issues going on around in us. The repetitive, nagging and discursive thoughts, the resentments, hurt, rejection, greed, desire, anger and bitterness are relentless. There is no room for expansion in this state. The mind that perpetually repeats itself in its own neurosis cannot just stop and do something different, the grooves are too well trodden.

The tragedy is that this mental play is considered to be normal. We become exhausted by maintaining our dramas and thinking patterns – 'My mind is so busy it is driving me crazy!' – as if this were some sort of achievement. In order to reinforce these patterns we surround ourselves with people who think and feel the same way. It is a basic human need to feel loved and to feel that we belong, so as long as there are others out there supporting and agreeing with us we feel safe!

Such confused activity in our heads locks us into a prison. We become not only out of touch with the world around us – able to see only that which lies right in front of us and not the greater picture – but we are also out of touch with what is happening in our hearts. The native Americans are known to have said, when first encountering the white man, that they could not understand him as, 'The white man thinks with his head instead of his heart.' We do not know how to think with our intuitive, feeling and caring qualities for we see these as being weak, instead we focus on those aspects of the mind that appear clever, rational and intellectually safe. To enter into the heart involves opening ourselves to a new way of being – and to stepping outside of the prison.

This takes insight and the willingness to be different. It may not happen until we are thrown into a vulnerable or irrational state – perhaps due to intense shock, illness or pain, or when we see our lives seemingly falling apart – for then the world beyond the superficial mind is glimpsed, we go deeper and penetrate the world of the heart. At first there may be a feeling of being broken hearted or tender hearted, but this crack can widen to true understanding.

Such traumatic experiences do not fit into the carefully constructed images life has built. They remove the reference points that have sustained our world and leave a groundlessness that relates to nothing solid. They defy rationality and we are catapulted into a different perspective. However, this enables us to see beyond ourselves, to discover a greater vision, not just one confined to our own self-centred viewpoint, but one that is of the whole.

The Wheel of Life

In the teachings of Tibetan Buddhism we find a picture that exemplifies the mind's image of the world when caught in such a basic self-centred nature as we have been discussing. It is the Wheel of Life, where all the various stages and forms of life are depicted, as well as the different states of confusion and chaos that we find ourselves in. This Wheel of Life is a vivid portrayal of the human dilemma, but it does not leave us as a helpless victim. Rather it shows us how to be able to leave behind such repetitive behaviour and enter into freedom.

Firstly, in the centre of the Wheel are three animals, each biting the tail of the one in front of it, thus forming a circle. This circle represents the very hub of human existence. The three animals are a pig, a cock and a snake. They symbolize the three basic root-causes of unenlightened (or unaware) existence which also contains all other states of delusion, and from which all limited causes arise. They are greed or desire, hatred or aversion, and delusion or ignorance.

The cock represents the greed, desire and attachment that we so love to crow about! It is this greed that dominates our material existence – the longing to possess both people and objects and to include these possessions in our world as a way of gaining a sense of security and safety. It is the desire for permanency and solidity, the lack of contentment with what is.

The snake embodies the hatred, enmity and aversion that is

The Tibetan Wheel of Life
(Illustration by Dharmachari Aloka, from *A Guide to the Buddhist Path* by Sangharakshita, Windhorse Publications.)

constantly poisoning us, creating wars, fighting and bitterness. This is the desire to be rid of that which is distasteful, so that we may feel secure and safe without such things. Whether they be people or objects, it makes no difference.

The pig symbolizes the darkness of unawareness, the instinctive urges and blindness that keep us maintaining our self-centred attitudes. This is the refusal or inability to be open-minded and to learn about anything which may create a threat to our carefully constructed security and safety. Thus we are closed to other ways of being, prejudiced towards other races and cultures. It is the belief that we are all separate and different, therefore an ignorance of the essential unity of all life.

These are quite a threesome! They represent the consciousness of the lower chakras, the instinctual and desirous nature that so dominates us. These three lead to confusion, indulgence, guilt, self-obsession and anxiety. If we can deal with their manifestations within us then we have conquered the deepest of all limitations, for from these arise all other fears and neuroses.

The Six Realms

In the next circle out from the centre are depicted six realms, each one representing a different aspect of existence. These realms are maintained by the delusion of separate self, for when we are able to go beyond such a delusion then there is no more duality, no more ignorance or separation, therefore no different realms of being.

Although each realm is showing the limitations of our delusions, there is also in each one a manifestation of the Buddha – representing the enlightened mind – who appears offering a specific means for salvation for those who wish to follow it. If we do follow then we are able to leave behind the self-perpetuating madness that so engulfs us.

The Gods

The first realm is the land of the gods where all desires and sensory pleasures are immediately satisfied. This is a beautiful place, soft and purely delightful, a true heaven. It is filled with music and dance, overflowing banquet tables and prolific, brilliantly coloured flowers. There is no pain or suffering, no ill health, just supreme happiness, beauty and longevity. Everything we could wish for is there, endlessly fulfilling our sensory delights.

However, indulgence in such pleasure also creates a forgetfulness that this type of bliss is not a permanent state – we easily become deluded into thinking that it is eternal! Both hope and fear diminish, as well as the reality of life and our purpose for being. The amnesia of bliss is so strong that we believe we have overcome the laws of the universe that tell us nothing ever stays the same. Here is where the limitations of existence are forgotten: the sufferings of other beings, the impermanence of all life. It is a blindness, a lack of awareness of the fact that this level of satisfaction does not last and therefore has no depth, no ultimate reality, but is merely a temporary plaything.

If the awareness of impermanence does arise, then we may start to lose faith in this haven, to get irritated and frustrated, even angry. How could we be let down in this way? We are being treated with injustice and it must be stopped! There is a fight to hold on to everything we have, even as it is slipping away from us.

The engrossing nature of this realm supports the illusion, keeping us blinded and unaware of a deeper experience – one that encompasses both pleasure and pain, one that reaches a spiritual magnitude. Therefore the Buddha appears here with a lute, using the music to awaken the occupants to the sounds of enlightenment. For these sounds are far more beautiful than any that may be heard by man, even in this heavenly realm of ecstasy. They are the sounds of our true divine Self, sounds that are sweeter than the furthest reaches of our imagination.

The Asuras

Next to the realm of the gods is the realm of the *asuras*, the warring titans or anti-gods. Here the language is one of war, violence, aggression and conflict. This realm depicts that aspect of humankind that is self-centred and deluded, drunk with jealousy and strife. It is the realm of paranoia, of plotting and planning. There is no compassion or understanding of the nature of reality here, there is simply the desire to fight, to assert and to dominate. Any form of communication is seen as either oppression or an attempt to take over. It is the realm obsessed with power, a greedy state as victory is desired at any cost. And rather than using this energetic response for the benefit of all beings, it is used to perpetuate ignorance, pain and separation.

Here the Buddha appears with a flaming sword. The sword is of the language the titans are familiar with, but the Buddha uses it not to cut through another person's throat, but to cut through our own delusion and confusion. It is wielded with love not hate. He teaches how the greater struggle, the more important assertion, is the one for knowledge and wisdom, for contentment and compassion, for victory over the senses not over each other.

The Pretas

Most of us are so immersed in desires and delusions that we cannot see beyond them. Therefore, next to the realm of the asuras is the realm of the *pretas* or hungry ghosts. Here the level of consciousness is consumed with unsatisfied passions, constantly wanting more and never finding fulfilment, confronted by limitations and the inability to share. Rather than longing for liberation, the mind is filled with a lust that keeps it bound to the physical realm. The preoccupation is with getting, yet fundamentally the inner feeling is one of poverty for there never seems to be enough. Pretas are depicted as having huge starving bellies with thin necks and tiny mouths and everything that is eaten turns to fire, so no matter how much food is consumed the longing within is never satisfied.

This is to show how every attempt to satisfy our passions and desires simply leads to more desire and thus to more pain. If everything in life is seen only in terms of possessing and owning then we will constantly be searching for distraction or fulfilment. Yet nothing is ever truly satisfying. It is an endless cycle. Here the Buddha appears carrying spiritual food and drink which, if we have the courage to swallow, will not only satisfy the longing and put out the fire, but will also enable us to transform the craving for worldly desires to divine ones.

The Hot Hell

Next to the hungry ghosts, and opposite to the heavenly abode of the gods, is the realm of infernal pain. This is the realm of hatred and anger, of a heat burning inside that turns all things hot. This heat makes everything feel claustrophobic and overwhelming. Here there is suffering and confusion, not as a form of God-given punishment but as a result of selfish and harmful actions. It is inevitable that those actions born out of aggression and fear will bring further pain, for we cannot lash out and hurt someone without hurting or being hurt ourselves. Cause and effect are one and the same – our anger with another ultimately poisons ourselves.

This is where Yama resides – the Judge of the Dead and the King of the Law – who simply holds up a mirror. It is the mirror of conscience in which our own behaviour is reflected back, giving us the opportunity to see ourselves objectively. This mirror can be our salvation, for from the pits of despair we can rise upwards again. In this way suffering can become a great cleanser, purifying delusion and enabling the true nature of reality to be seen. Many of us will be familiar with the growth and understanding that emerges from times of pain and turmoil. For suffering can break the illusion of permanency and solidity and put us in touch with the reality of impermanence and selflessness.

In this realm there is therefore the choice of being able to grow and transcend ignorance and suffering; or we can become so self-centred that we are obsessed with the pain, endlessly perpetuating it in order to hold on to a familiar security. Here the Buddha appears holding a purifying flame, that which can bring eternal light to our darkness.

The Animals

Next to the hell realm and opposite to the asuras is the realm of fear and ignorance, depicted by animals. This realm is dominated by instinctive and habitual reaction; of the need to be a part of a group rather than being able to stand out as an individual; of a constant preoccupation with survival; of a fear so deep that all things are seen as a potential enemy; of an ignorance of anything beyond the immediate reality. Here there is no thought of higher wisdom, for we have no ability to discriminate or to reflect. There is simply mindless and repeated activity, an obsession with basic survival. It is a form of stupidity in the sense that there is no innovation, simply repetitive behaviour; it is also a blindness that sees no other way of being except our own. There is no conception of anything beyond ourselves.

From the animals has emerged humankind with the added ability to think, thus creating individuation and potential. Therefore the Buddha appears here with a book in his hands, representing the teachings – the dharma – or the path that leads us from such a state of ignorance to one of wisdom.

Humankind

Between the realms of the gods and the animals is the realm of humankind. This is the realm of the desire and searching for happiness, the constant quest for fulfilment, which differs from the desire in the hell realm as there is the added quality of selective intelligence. For here we seek the higher aspirations, the higher ideals. Thus there is an emphasis on learning and education, on the acquiring of knowledge, the development of the intellect. Eventually this can lead us beyond the realms of suffering and beyond our limitations to ultimate liberation and pure wisdom. It is only when we begin to traverse the spiritual path, to enquire into the nature of reality and what lies beyond it, that we become truly human. Before then we are animals, we are titans, we are deluded gods, or we are suffering and in torment.

The Buddha appears here as a wandering mendicant with his begging bowl and staff, indicative of a being who has gone beyond the limitations of a selfish and egotistical mind, to that of selflessness and egolessness. This is the being who has merged into and is one with the awakened mind and is pointing the way to the freedom that we can all experience.

From this graphic description we can see the many realms of existence we experience. We may move from one state to another over a period of time, we may even experience all of them in one day, or we may get stuck in one for a lifetime! All six realms are within us: the bliss of the god realm, the jealousy and aggression of the titans, the greed and meanness of the hungry ghosts, the anger and pain of the hell realm, the ignorance and fear of the animals, and the searching for happiness in the human realm. It is not difficult to recognize ourselves or others in any of these portrayals: the mad general intent on war, the self-obsessed millionaire living in luxury, the bankrupt and the lonely, the starving and the searching. In seeing the levels of ignorance that perpetuate these states, we also see how rare is the desire for higher truth, greater understanding and true liberation, how so few actually make the effort to get off the wheel.

Inter-dependence

At the outer rim of the Wheel of Life we find what are known as the twelve links of dependent origination or co-arising. This describes how every action and every thing is dependent on and inter-related to something else, that there is nothing that arises free of this dependency. The importance of understanding this is because it shows us how we cannot separate ourselves from each other, cannot think we are without relationship to all other things. As the author Anne Bancroft says in *The Spiritual Journey*, 'Dependent co-arising is a vision of reality as dynamic relativity, a process of inter-existence and interdependence in which the doer and the deed, the person and the environment, are mutually causative.' In other words we are all reflected in and connected to each other as well as to all other things. Each plays its own unique part, being both a cause and an effect. The outer circle of the Wheel depicts this co-dependency by showing the movement of creation.

The twelve pictures start with an image of a blind woman feeling her way with a stick. This represents our spiritual blindness or unawareness, the ignorance at the base of our existence. We create our own illusions and imaginings of this world, as we stumble through it, blind to its true nature.

Our character is thus formed according to the nature of our will, action and motivation, and this is represented by the second picture, a potter making a pot on his wheel. As he moulds a pot out of raw materials, so we create our reality, forming a life out of our attitudes and ignorance. This is known as volitional action.

Out of this primal ignorance arises consciousness, repre-sented here by a monkey grasping a branch. Our blind igno-rance gives rise to restlessness and in the same way that a monkey leaps from branch to branch, so our mind is never still, never satisfied, it is constantly leaping from one thing to another.

However, consciousness needs a form in which to material-ize, a means for expression. The fourth link is therefore the mind and body combination, the emergence of form (body) and the means for that form to be expressed (mind). This is depicted by a boat with two people in it.

From the body and mind arise the six senses (the five senses and our mind that senses mental objects) which are our means of perception. This is represented as a house with six windows, for it is through our senses that we perceive the world and bring that perception to consciousness.

The senses then make contact with their object, shown in the sixth picture as the image of two lovers. This gives rise to sense-impression. Dependent upon contact arises feeling and sensation. This is seen in the image of a blind man with his eye pierced by an arrow, depicting sensation so great that it blinds us to reality and we no longer see our way clearly.

Feelings give rise to desire – to a great thirst. This is

represented by a man being served a drink. It is the thirst for life, the hunger for more, the endless flame of desire. But this longing can also give rise to pain, clinging and attachment, seen in the image of a man gathering fruit in a basket, filling the basket beyond what he could possibly need. And as we saw earlier, from clinging arises desire and sexual pleasure. The next picture is therefore of a man and woman in sexual embrace, or of a pregnant woman.

Naturally this leads to birth and the next picture is that of a child being born. But from life also comes death and the last picture shows a dead man being carried to the graveyard. This reminds us that all life is impermanent, will come and go. And so back we come to the blind lady, for is it not our ignorance of separate selfhood that is perpetuating this round of life and death?

The Realm of Absurdity

Being trapped in the mind is like being trapped in the delusions of those realms described above. They become overwhelming and all encompassing, they are our daily reality. Yet there is also another realm that the Wheel of Life does not depict and that is the realm of absurdity!

The absurd mind is totally self-absorbed. It is the mind that starts telling its story and then continually repeats itself, over-indulging in its own paranoia. The absurd mind believes that itself and this world are real and substantial, it cannot see the lack of substantiality and the total impermanence of all things. The absurd mind is locked in a cage yet believes itself to be free, is in a paper bag yet thinks it can see in all directions. The absurd mind is immersed in trivia and pettiness, making mountains out of molehills. It is a nagging despot, always needing to be right.

In this realm the mind is constantly creating fearful scenarios that are beyond the present moment. Have you ever noticed how absurd it is that we spend so much time worrying about something that hasn't happened yet, and may not even happen at all? Yet we spend hours, even days, in fear of what could happen! We are so anxious about the future that we cannot live in the present.

The mind that can see this absurdity but does not know how to deal with it may become mad, become crazed with a vision but without the means to put that vision into perspective, for there is no anchor or reference point. We all have the potential for madness, for we can see and reach beyond our limitations if we so choose. With such a vision we either accept the irrational or we are thrown into chaos. Often those who do become clinically mad are experiencing visions and a deep insight into reality, they simply have no context in which to understand these insights. The resulting conflict is due to a confusion of what is real and what is unreal. This conflict can lead to madness.

The yogis or awakened ones see the absurdity of life but are not bound by it. Although they experience the same events as others they see through the confusion and are free of personal involvement. They know there is nothing permanent and that the madness of the mundane world is actually groundless. There is no reference point other than awakened consciousness. By coming out of the chaotic mind and into the heart we connect with the true reality of existence. Hence we go beyond the insanity to acceptance and compassion. Perhaps this is the real meaning of insanity: that to be in-sane is to be sane within. For here the absurd mind and the insubstantial nature of life are seen as an illusion and thus are not in conflict.

Being out of our mind usually implies, as Alan Watts said in *Meditation*, '. . . thoughtlessness, mindlessness, unthinking, empty-headed and vagueness. . . . Perhaps this is some measure of an innate fear of releasing the chronic cramp of consciousness by which we grasp the facts of life and manage the world.' However, the state we are looking at here is not one of mindlessness but rather of mindfulness, one of finding a freedom from the confines of the habitual mind, a freedom not constrained or hidden behind a paper bag. The state we are talking about enables spontaneous, creative and even irrational qualities to be embraced.

This implies that as we come out of our minds we begin to understand the nature of reality. It means that we are willing to feel, to communicate, to go beyond our fixations and fears, to a place of personal awareness – to come out of the paper bag and the false protection it provides. For we will remain a victim of our own limitations until we are able to embrace and honour who we really are. If we do not recognize our own issues they will dominate and influence us – we become a victim of that which we have not gained mastery over.

The conditioned mind offers little change, it is compelled to act out of habit. Only by being brave warriors can we use the sword of insight to cut through this surface superficiality of conditioning to a free and energetic state. This willingness allows the heart to open to a deeper, more sensitive and aware way of being. It is an awakening to the joy of unlimited potential.

2

The Haunting Ghost of the Ever-Demanding Ego!

The ego is probably the most complex and confusing aspect of the mind, yet in reality it is an illusion! The ego is our sense of individuality, it creates the image of who we think we are with all our elusive and erratic qualities. It is defensive, secret and covetous, yet also aggressive and demanding. The ego is all the me's and mine's, the 'I' that gets into every crevice of our lives. It makes us think we are either real or pretend, substantial or insubstantial, important or unimportant. The ego fills us with the false confidence of believing we are greater than another, the desire to grasp for ourselves, to hurt or deny others, to think we are always right; equally it can make us believe we are weak or wrong, that we lack confidence and are a nobody. It is that which reacts to success and happiness as a boost to our importance, then reacts with self-pity when things go wrong.

As Dzigar Kongtrul Rinpoche explains in *The Depths of Your Mind*,

> The function of the ego is to bring forth passion, aggression, jealousy and pride ... We give the nature of the body and the mind a ... permanence which makes it solid and rigid. But it is not so. Living within that idea brings forth a passion for it. Then, if the passion is not evolved, aggression comes out of it. And because of that there is a 'self' and 'others' and jealousy becomes involved.

Most of us are led to believe that it is necessary to have an ego – to have passion and aggression – in order to make our

The Haunting Ghost of the Ever-Demanding Ego!

way in the world, for without it we are seen as being spineless, weak and undeveloped. Indeed, there are doubtless times when there is a need to boost the ego – to develop greater assertion and confidence – especially if we have been severely battered or bruised by life. If we think we have no value or self-worth, how can we discover a sense of identity? However, it is not as if we should or should not have an ego, rather it is our attitude towards it that we need to look at.

For the ego plays the most intricate and subtle games and it takes keen insight and awareness to recognize these! This is especially so as we begin to take our spiritual journey more seriously. Why are we practising meditation, or learning different healing techniques, or giving to the poor? Is it so that we feel better? Do we want to be something special, to stand out as someone to be respected and revered? What is our personal investment? Finding the answers is not easy, it demands being very honest with ourselves. Do we really want to be free? It is natural to voice our desire for freedom, for no one *wants* to be confined. But, deep inside, is freedom our primary goal? In other words, is our motivation one of serving the ego, or is it to go beyond the ego?

Checking our actions means becoming observant but without being critical of what we find. If we see ego-centred or disrupting aspects we should not be angry or filled with remorse and guilt, that not only gets us nowhere fast but just adds further negativity. Instead, can we be clear about our real objectives? Can we find how much resentment really lies beneath our good intentions? As we happily clean the toilets, are we actually feeling annoyed because no one else has offered to do it? When we visit the elderly or the sick, are we relieved when we come to leave that at last our good deed for the day is now done? This questioning should not be merely an intellectual assignment! For here we are not talking about the mind with all its rationality and clever answers, but about how we feel within our hearts.

In questioning our motivation, we need to ask if we are ready to have nothing to complain about. To have no specific reason why people should pay us attention. Can we see ourselves without our limitations? If we can accept the faults in others and still love them, can we not do the same with ourselves? Our difficulties (whether physical or psychological) tend to give us a feeling of distinction, they act as our credentials, in making us appear different they keep us separate. Eventually they become the focal point in our lives, determining our actions, creating an excuse for our behaviour and giving us endless causes for complaint. We are suffering and we want everyone else to know about it! But how would it feel to be just ordinary, without having anything special about us?

The ego makes us believe we are *something*, that this something is different and special, and that it is separate from everything and everyone else. Maintaining this sense of specialness and separation is the ego's way of maintaining itself, for when we become aware of our essential unity and oneness with all beings the ego is out of its job! It will therefore do whatever it has to in order to perpetuate its employment.

The Ghost of Delusion

In glorifying the ego we have glorified a false reality. As Khentin Tai Situpa says in *Way to Go*,

> The ego is the real demon that persecutes us; a completely non-existent demon since, no matter how hard we search, it can never be found as anything. Nevertheless, once the illusory belief in a self has been created then that 'I' desires its happiness, resents suffering and is ignorant of the actual way in which true happiness can be found. . . . All the sufferings we have at present are the result of our own past unskillful attempts to satisfy the ego or protect it from unhappiness.

A ghost is that which we sense is there but can't quite see, yet things get changed and we don't know how. In the same way the elusive ego is there, like a ghost we can sense but never quite grasp, yet is always influencing and affecting our lives. And we are so used to the ghost being there that we cannot imagine being without it! Life would feel somehow empty.

The ego has this strong influence because of the belief that we are all independent from each other. For the delusion that the ego is creating is this false sense of separation. It is the belief that only 'I' is important, that me and mine must come before us and ours. How often do we say, 'I come first,' or 'What about me?' If any of this sounds familiar, do not be surprised! The ego-centred state is indigenous to humankind, reflected in all walks of life. It is as if we are given this cross to bear and to overcome, for the ego is the battle with ourselves. In order to find *real* peace we have to see through and become free of the influence it has, to cut through the layers of delusion rather than be bound.

As we evolve in consciousness we move from the animal-like state of preservation and survival to developing our own identity as a separate individual. In the process we become more self-centred and focused on the ego. The next step is the development of the true individual – one who experiences no separation between self and other – and is therefore egoless. It is like looking at the dust on a mirror. We see the dust and identify with this as our reflection, when in fact the dust is hiding the true clarity of our image beneath it. The more we identify with the dust – which represents the deluded reflection of ourselves created by the ego – the less we see the true image. When we emerge out of this delusion into a state of freedom we become one with that image.

The Third Chakra

This level of ego-defined individuality relates to the consciousness of the second and third chakras. The second we have already discussed as the primary consciousness of desire and greed. The relevance of this to the ego is obvious for the very nature of the ego is to serve the self first, to have the world revolving around our own personal needs and desires. We are immersed in pleasure and pain, when we don't get what we want then we get angry, depressed, or see it as a confirmation of our hopelessness. The consciousness of the second chakra is of an unrefined nature, there is no true discrimination or self-awareness. With the emergence of third chakra consciousness the ego begins to become more refined and precise, to develop in relation to others. This indicates the development of consciousness from the more primal type of qualities – those of survival and reproduction – to the more clearly human ones of discrimination, awareness and choice. This is the core of ego-identity, particularly of power and manipulation. We expand our basic greed to seek domination and control, especially over others.

The consciousness of this chakra generates concern about whether we are liked or disliked, will be accepted or not, whether we are superior or inferior. More energy is invested into our image and how we appear to others. We may project a big image even if we feel small inside or vice versa. For instance, feeling inferior and insignificant, lacking confidence or believing others know better can be just as ego-centred as feelings of grandiosity and superiority, of being all-powerful and a great achiever. Both attitudes are concerned with self and the effect of self on our world, they imply an obsession with self.

The third chakra indicates the emergence of the ego in this most self-centred form as we search for validation, for a means to exert ourselves and to control the events in our lives. There may be extreme obeisance or, equally, little respect for the feelings or wishes of others, and even less for those who think differently from us. Intolerance, irritation, frustration, manipulation and deception are key attitudes here. So also is self-belief. When there is a strong and very dominant power-filled ego it creates within us the conviction that we are right, over and above others. There can be no other way. How can someone else be right when I know I am?

For instance, how many times has a simple little incident between two lovers or partners sparked off a painful or angry argument? If we could manage to be a fly on the wall at any one such incident (or better still, tape the event to be played back later when objectivity is possible!) we would see how amusing the situation really is. When we enter into a close relationship with another person the boundaries of the two egos sort of melt and merge, creating a whole between the two people. When we are in harmony, this is wonderful. But all too often the experience of such deep intimacy can be overwhelming and we pull back into ourselves a little. When we do that the egos get re-formed in their separate identities. However, they are still very close so there is a natural tendency for them to start bumping into each other, thus creating conflict while all the time searching for union!

Go back to being the fly on the wall, and we will clearly see one ego holding on tight for dear life against another ego doing exactly the same. If we see this the argument soon loses all meaning and relevance! The real problem is not the original cause of the argument at all but rather the need each one of us has to be right – it is the inability to surrender our own point of view to another. The only way out of this, quickly and without damage, is to have the courage to see the ridiculousness of it all and to laugh! To just laugh, thus releasing all the tension. By letting go of the hold the ego has it then enables others to do the same.

Eddie remembers many years ago, when he was a monk in India and he was learning how to work through this egocentric mind that always has to be right. His teacher, Paramahamsa Satyananda, tried to explain, 'When I am right and you are wrong, then it is easy for you to accept my being right. But when I am wrong and you are right and you are able to surrender your need to be right, then you are surrendering the ego.' Surrender helps us break through the rigidity of the rational mind, the fixity and inability to compromise. It opens us up to a whole new way of being, one in which there is flexibility and spontaneity. However, being egoless does not mean that we have to give up everything and become a monk! What it does mean is simply being at ease with ourselves and with what is, without making demands or drawing attention to ourselves. There is a spaciousness beyond the limitations.

The Use of Power

The power trips the ego leads us into often appear as fun, despite the fact that they inevitably include pain. It is therefore not easy to see through the ego, it has a wonderful way of screening us from reality. It is like a horse wearing blinkers – we can't see in all directions, only straight in front of us. We are taught how to overpower others, how to get what we want and how to win, how might makes right. But we are not taught how to be sensitive and gentle. Is this why nations are so aggressive in the name of freedom? Why we believe we have to fight wars in order to have peace? The dominance of the third chakra energy convinces us that power is freedom and control is beneficial as it keeps order intact; we believe we know best and are able to lead others in the right direction.

In the political field it is easy to see how consciousness manifests at this level of power, creating the personality that can head a country yet can lie or deceive without hesitation, can manipulate events and evade questions about difficult or revealing topics. Here the need is for power and domination not just in our own world, but in a larger arena where we can project our own beliefs outwards. Now at last the world will recognize us for the brilliant and supreme being we know we are!

This is a misuse of power as it is combined with the intellect rather than the heart. We see it in many of the world's leaders who have manipulated and deceived so many people, yet have done it because they firmly believed what they were doing to be right. Hitler is a perfect example of a very strong ego illusion at this level. He had no doubt that he was right and he just had to convince the rest of the world. He believed that by using domination and violence it would prove his rightness, that he would be seen as the true world leader he so believed himself to be.

Throughout the ages the Church has been notorious for its pilfering and misuse of funds, for the power it has wielded over king and country. It has ruled governments and shaped the way the world developed. Nowadays, the Church is perhaps beginning to listen to the needs of the people, to become more reflective and less manipulative, although change is still needed in many areas. We are also seeing power issues with some of the gurus and cults that have emerged in the later half of this century, that have led to the disempowering of the followers – of their personal judgement and understanding – in favour of the guru. An extreme example is that of the cult leader Jim Jones who incited his followers to commit mass suicide at their Jonestown community in Guyana.

Although suicide is an extreme action to take, the giving of our power to another (to God, the guru, or whoever) is not uncommon. It implies we do not trust ourselves enough to make decisions or to take responsibility, a state that is not surprising considering the emotional difficulties so many of us grew up experiencing. Rather we believe that someone else – especially someone who appears so self-assured – must know better than we do. Many people function on the unaware level of the second chakra and less have evolved the power or control aspects of the third chakra, so the many follow the few leaders and we find that the 'power is in the hands of the few'.

We see a similar scenario in the world of channelling or mediumship. Here the person who is the channel steps aside, as it were, to allow the entity to speak through him or her.

This can be seen as a tremendous act of egolessness, a great sacrifice in order that the teachings of this entity may come through to benefit us all. Yet is that always the case? Is it not possible that such stepping aside can also indicate little trust or faith in our own understanding – therefore the need to look to another for wisdom rather than claiming our own – as much as it can be a sign of a well-developed ego? For look at the praise the channels get, that they are the ones chosen to receive the entity. And how easy it is, when in this position, not to have to take any responsibility for what occurs, for surely it is the entity speaking, not the channel.

We are not implying that channelling is either right or wrong, and certainly not that all channels can be described in this way. Simply that each one of us needs to be honest with ourself and clear in our communication, to look deeply inside and find out who *we* are and what our own wisdom is.

The right use of power is not easy, it takes skill and sensitivity. The ego-centred level of power we have been discussing here creates the character of leadership but it can also have a destructive effect. It is far more ego-fulfilling to get lured into power of a manipulative form, for the world is structured in such a way that we believe that to dominate is the ultimate answer. We worship power as if it were a god, for were we not told that 'man shall have dominion over the earth'? When we finally have true domination over others, whether it be our children, our lovers, or a whole group of people, then it appears as if we have achieved a great goal.

The need to reach the top of the mountain, to accomplish our desires and be successful, is the natural impulse to move towards experiencing greater happiness. The difficulty lies in believing that success means being all-powerful; we forget that there is a difference between being powerful in the sense of being egotistic and controlling, and being powerful meaning full of divine love or cosmic power. True power is not corruptive or abusive, it transcends greed and serves for the benefit of others. This is where the fourth chakra begins to awaken – the opening of the heart. Success in this context does not mean the domination over others but over ourselves, over our own lower nature: our greed, fear, selfishness, jealousy and anger.

If we are able to recognize the limitations of the ego and not get so entrapped, then we will be able to realize the deeper level of consciousness of the third chakra. For from personal power we can move to understanding power for the good of all, of seeing the value of all viewpoints, of true service and sharing. The ego is only a ruling master as long as it is not recognized for what it is. We have the ability to change, to evolve, to see through the limitations. While the world is seen as a powerful reality and we are focused on what we can get out of it, then we are caught in the illusion. But if we can see beyond ourselves to that which connects us all, then our lives can have a very different emphasis and our higher purpose can become a living reality.

Fear of Freedom

However, the ego not only keeps us fixed in our delusions but it also makes us believe we are not good enough to deserve freedom, are not of such a calibre, could not possibly realize the essence of existence! Are we not just humble mortals, beginners on the journey with a long way to go before we come anywhere near to being free?

How extraordinary it is that we believe we are so limited that we cannot be enlightened! To think that we cannot become free, when freedom is our natural state! We believe we are the dust on the mirror and could never be so beautiful as the reflection beneath the dust. Yet are we really so special that our problems are bigger than someone else's? Do we, perhaps, cling to sickness? Are we actually afraid of healing? Do we cling to our limitations? Are we fearful of freedom? What is it that makes us believe we cannot realize great wisdom and insight ourselves, but have to go to someone else to find it? Surely we are also worthy of such insight?

The haunting ghost of the ego is that which is always there, prodding and influencing us, stimulating our motivation and actions, creating dramas and crisis. Am I nice enough? Am I too nice? Some people find it embarrassing to express love and even more so to love themselves. Modesty is certainly an important characteristic, but is such a lack of expression not a play of the ego? Inhibitions hold us back for fear of appearing foolish. By keeping us in doubt and confusion, the ego distracts us from seeing our true nature. Mocking us, then making us think we are great – the pendulum swings and we are the game. Becoming free of the ego implies becoming free of this obsession with ourselves. It also implies that we do not cling to the dust on the mirror!

One of the feelings we may encounter as we begin to recognize this state of resistance to freedom in ourselves is a fear of what lies ahead if we do manage to experience egolessness. We may believe we have overcome our fear of physical death and know that it is not as terrifying or bad as we had thought. But what we are now encountering is the fear of the death of the ego. The future has always appeared to be fearful – what tomorrow holds for us is unknown and brings to mind too many unanswerable possibilities. To face this future without our normal guidelines and reference points is almost unthinkable.

Is it possible to become fearless and let go of the ego all at once? We have created such a strong image of ourselves and do everything we can in order to protect this image, so it seems inconceivable to be able to let go of it. How can we let go of something we believe we are? As Dzigar Kongtrul Rinpoche says, 'You must challenge the ego. This is fearful because you are going from the known to the unknown. You have spent a lifetime creating that ego, that you. To now let go of it, then what do you have?'

The fear of being free is the fear of letting go of all the props and thought patterns that we have lived with and maintained over the years. Even the skeletons in the closet are familiar skeletons; we feel a strange sense of comfort knowing they are there, despite their ugliness they are at least familiar! Letting them go is not such a reassuring idea. How would it feel to have an empty closet? We fear the death of our ego because it is what has built us, has created the very fabric of our being. Who will we be if we go beyond the ego, to a state of egolessness and freedom? If we let go of our sack of antiques? Will we be the same person, and if not, then who? Will we still be able to function, to work, to make love, to have what we need? We have lived with our limitations for so long that we may feel naked without them.

An Inner Revolution

We cannot escape the experience of the ego and its effects until we begin to awaken to self-awareness. For the ego keeps us in a state of separation not just from others, but also from God, from that within us that is free. The ego is that which is not in touch with or acting from God consciousness. We are all equally capable of tremendous insight and wisdom, but the ego nature denies it, convincing us we are too ignorant and limited for such lofty aims, making us believe we are not good enough. We need a revolution within in order to overthrow this ego-belief – a revolution in which we challenge the ego!

We are easily led away from the truth into a state that appears to be solid ground, to be permanent. We believe that who and what we are is real, for as long as we are self-involved we are involved with the ego. If we do not question the ego nature then this idea of solidity eventually leads to aggression and passion as it is a false reality that cannot sustain itself; but if we can look more deeply by observing the ego then the possibility for generosity and compassion emerges. When we realize we are knocking our heads against the wall – when the fruitlessness of our actions is seen – then the ego starts to crack. The ghost behind us, yet always with us, will remain in control until we are ready to turn around and face it!

How rare it is to meet someone who is genuinely giving, without thought for themselves, for it takes tremendous letting go and surrender to realize the wisdom of emptiness, the reality of impermanence. Here is someone who has mastered a successful revolution! Yet when we do meet such a person we usually greet them with either awe or doubt, for there are no familiar reference points. We know how to relate to the ego and all its appearances, but how to relate to egolessness? To a state of complete openness, fearlessness, compassion and wisdom all rolled into one? We associate this with

God or sainthood, in so doing we subordinate ourselves and put them above us. Or we think they must be a fake, for no one can be that perfect! It is much easier to doubt the validity and motivation of such a person than it is to confront in ourselves that which is holding us back from being similarly free. Do we not trust it because we do not trust ourselves?

Although the ego creates the illusion of our reality – all the ups and downs, the happy and unhappy moments – it may also be the very tool we can use to go beyond it. How wonderful when we learn to say e-go! As Khentin Tai Situpa points out in *Way To Go,*

> It is not as if the ego is bad – that we should hate it and fight it. Rather it is a pointless delusion that has caused trouble and its removal comes through understanding, penetrating through to the essence of existence. We do not need to hate it but use it, to make it the seed of realization . . . This is the proper revolution.

If we can observe the way the ego works in ourselves, the suffering it brings and the effect it has on our lives, so we can also see how others are affected by ego, how that same impulse is in them too. Actions and behaviour that seem so selfish or confused can be seen to be arising from a place of illusion, of belief in separation and an ignorance of oneness. Only when we believe we are separate from each other does selfishness arise. If we realize this then we can generate real compassion and a deeper understanding of human nature. We may even be able to understand abuse or anger by recognizing how the abuser is locked into his or her own pain and is searching for release. The abuse usually has little to do with the one being abused. Such understanding is an essential part of the ego-revolution.

It is not as if we should deny our pain or the abuse we may have experienced. However, we can work with it so that it does not have such a strong influence in our lives. Pain is inevitable, we are fragile beings and can easily be hurt. But suffering is not synonymous with pain. Suffering is when we carry the pain beyond its natural time. For instance, if some-one we are close to dies and we argued with them just before-hand, or perhaps we were not there when it happened, then the pain of the death is compounded by our actions and we may continue to feel guilty – to suffer – for many years to come. The suffering we experience seems to somehow redeem our actions. The pain of loss is natural, but the suffering prolongs that pain, thus alleviating the guilt. We cannot change the past, cannot change anything that has ever happened, nor can we change anyone else, but we can change our attitude. Most especially, we can forgive ourselves and let go.

There is a wonderful story of two Buddhist monks who are walking together and come to a river. Standing on the edge of the river is a beautiful young woman. She is unable to walk across the river and begs the monks to help her. One of them picks her up and carries her across, putting her down on the opposite bank before walking on. After a few miles the second monk suddenly bursts out saying, 'You know we are not meant to touch women! You have broken the rules! How could you do that? How could you pick her up like that?' The first monk replies quietly, 'I left her at the river bank. Are you still carrying her?'

Although our worries and needs are so influenced by the ego, so it can also be the ego that begins to demand a greater level of happiness than the merely superficial one we are so used to. In other words, the ego can actually be responsible for our taking the first steps on our spiritual journey, pushing us to achieve a state of greater calm or relaxation, a kinder nature or a more loving disposition. It is, at the same time, both our worst enemy as through it is created all manner of suffering, and also our best friend as it can be the stimulus for us to start seeking greater freedom. So it is not as if the ego were simply bad, or is to be denied or destroyed. It may create untold chaos and confusion, but working with these conditions is the very path to egolessness.

Debbie remembers when she chose to do a six week solitary meditation retreat, away in the mountains. 'During the first week the difficulty of facing my complete aloneness was offset by my level of pride – I dare not lose face by not completing what I had set out to do! By the second week my love of being in retreat had become stronger than the desire to leave. Thus, the prideful ego served a useful purpose by making me stay where I was and therefore confront my aloneness.'

Our difficulties and limitations can thus become our stepping stones, we can use the energy of the ego to step across from ignorance to wisdom. We can even turn around and confront our ghost, for when a ghost is seen in the clear light of day it quickly vanishes! Eventually what we find is that, rather than the ego being done away with, it actually becomes redundant. It begins to get in the way of our communicating openly and freely, from being loving and generous, and as we change we want to express these egoless qualities more than we do the egotistic ones. The true revolution is one that quickly makes itself unnecessary!

The Six Hindrances

Traditionally there are six different characteristics that represent the predominant ways in which the ego expresses itself, and these are therefore the most immediate aspects we can start working with to bring about transformation. Through them we are able to reach all parts of the ego-nature. These characteristics are called the *six hindrances*.

Ignorance

Ignorance is the first of these six. What is meant by this is the ignorance that perpetuates narrow-minded and unaware states of mind. We tend to get so locked into our own way of thinking, believing that our way is the only way, that we deny the importance and validity of anything else. It can take great courage to open ourselves to how others feel when that feeling is different to ours, but if we do not then we stay imprisoned in a limited mind-set.

We were once being interviewed on the radio when a man phoned in to the programme. He said to us, 'You are saying that we can find peace within ourselves, that through relaxation and meditation we can find peace. Well, it's not true. Only through my teacher can we find peace. You believe that all religious paths should be honoured, well they should not. There is only one path.' The interesting point about this man's statement was that he may have been right – but only for him. He had found his path as through his faith he was finding what he believed to be peace. Yet his true freedom was being limited because he was negating any other possibility and was therefore stuck in his mind-set. By denying others he was denying his own freedom.

The ignorance this man was expressing was the lack of understanding that we all have different needs. No one way is better or worse than another, nor are all ways appropriate for all people. He was also failing to realize that his external teacher is, in essence, one and the same as his own true nature, and therefore his peace did actually lie inside himself and not through another person. As soon as there is prejudice against another or another's path, then this is the ignorance of our essential unity. Such prejudice eventually becomes an obstacle and prevents us from being free.

What we are talking about is therefore a lack of awareness of and discrimination between virtue and non-virtue. To be virtuous is to practise understanding, compassion, basic goodness and acceptance; it is to have grasped a sense of universal morality and to be willing to live by that. To be non-virtuous is to be closed, dismissive and uncaring, to be shut off from others, seeing them as a threat to the fabric of our own lives. This is the ego expressing its sense of separation, its inability to unite and be one with all.

Desire

The second of our six hindrances is desire and attachment. This is a root cause for so much of our suffering in life as we are constantly focused on wanting, getting, holding on to, and then experiencing pain when none of this happens or we lose what we have gained. It is humankind's prime condition – to want and to be looking for happiness – but it becomes translated as a greedy and desperate struggle for possessions, rather than a search for inner peace. We grow up conditioned to believe we have to be a success, make money, have all the things we desire, and that this is our true goal, this is fulfilment. Yet in practice it usually brings confusion, suffering and loss. We are constantly creating emotional programmes for happiness that do not work. What happens when we have it all but are still not happy?

This domination by desire is never ending. No matter how little or how much we have, it is never enough. It is interesting to note that often those people who have the least are more willing to share than those who have more than they could possibly use. Is it that we lose ourselves so much in what we have that we become identified with our possessions? Do we become fearful that others only want us because of what they can get from us? When we have very little we tend to be freer and able to let go. When we have a great deal we are in constant fear of losing it, so we forget how to share.

Attachment to our possessions is totally engrossing, even blinding. These possessions may be materialistic, may be our family, our children, or our career and accomplishments. We become equally attached to our fears and habitual patterns, holding on to them for support and security. We can even become as attached to our spiritual progress as we can to our progress in the world. Unless we are able to see the energy surrounding desire and attachment then we will simply transfer these tendencies to whatever activity we may be involved in, even if that is meditation or yoga.

There is a trend nowadays to think that enlightenment is something we can 'get', maybe by going to the right workshops or seminar intensives, or being with the right teacher. We are told that as long as we worship this particular person, practise this type of meditation, change our thinking patterns and only behave in a certain way, or maybe even subject ourselves to many hours of painful postures, then we will get something, ideally enlightenment. This approach to freedom implies a transference of our desires and attachments from the material realm to the non-material; it is the accumulation of spiritual materialism. It has distorted the true meaning of enlightenment, reducing it to implying little more than possessing a positive mental attitude.

The ego will naturally try to keep us in a greedy and desirous state of mind, but we can overcome this by seeing attachment for what it is, by seeing the constant round of pain and pleasure that desire brings and by releasing the control of such desire. To be free of wanting, to be doing something purely for its own sake, without any ulterior motive, is to be at peace. It is not that the awakened being lives in this world any differently than others, but the awakened state is not attached to results. A lack of desire does not mean a dead or indifferent state, rather it is an open and receptive one; to be free of attachments does not mean to be cold and uncaring, but instead we can be more giving, more caring, for we are not seeking anything in return. We can therefore give freely.

This is what is meant by discipline – the ability to develop control of our desires rather than their being in control of us. It is to see that the desire itself is not as important as the energy we give it, and that we can be creatively responsive rather than habitually reactive. If we can see discipline as constructive and productive, as an expression of our natural state and as a means to true freedom, then it can have real meaning in our lives.

One of Debbie's teachers once recounted a story of how a student had come to him saying that he no longer wished to meditate. When asked why, the student replied, 'Because I do not want to stop wanting things, and I know that if I continue meditating I will become detached to the point of not wanting anything.' The teacher laughed and replied, 'That's not quite how it works! Detachment does not mean that you stop wanting things. For instance, I still want warm clothes to wear, I still want good food and a roof over my head. I still enjoy the things of life. The difference is that if I don't get these things then it doesn't bother or upset me. I am still at peace.'

Anger

The third of the hindrances is anger or hatred. Here the ego erupts with emotion as it feels attacked and personally insulted. This shows another aspect of our separation from each other, for only by believing we are separate can we be so affected by someone else. If we were in a state of unity and egolessness we would be able to see the pain being experienced by the other person resulting in such anger and would realize that we were not the cause of the anger, simply the nearest and most convenient place to off-load it. The idea is not to always be drawing everything into ourselves and believing it has something to do with us, but rather seeing the bigger picture which includes all things.

Anger is very destructive, not only for the person receiving it, but also for ourselves. When we get angry it boosts our ego, making us feel right and important. We immediately lose touch with a greater vision – an image of the whole where we are just one part – and become engrossed in only our viewpoint. This is limiting and self-centred. It implies an inflexible and rigid attitude. Although there may be many good reasons why venting anger is psychologically beneficial, there are also traditional teachings warning us of the inherent dangers that arise as soon as we let anger have power. Its destructive nature has been described as a single match that can burn an entire forest of trees, for once anger has been voiced it is not easy to rebuild the resulting devastation.

Anger implies energy and we can transform that energy and use it for the benefit of all, rather than releasing it on just one. We can turn it into flexibility and openness. If we cannot deal with our anger directly, then let us at least try reducing it, maybe from five hours to four and then to three! It is not as if we should repress or stuff our anger away, but rather learn how to let go of it more quickly by seeing through the egotistic nature of it.

Hatred is another aspect of anger, combined with the ignorance we spoke about above. For hatred is against something, implying that we are in a conflict of ideals and cannot accept another's way of being. Throughout history wars have been started on less than this. It breaks up friendships and destroys our relationship to ourselves as well as to the world. It creates self-righteousness and discontent, at the same time as strengthening the ego. We believe we can hate someone or something without affecting ourselves.

Hatred will poison our system, filling our days with negative emotions that in turn affect our health and well-being. This destructive power affects all of creation. To cut hatred at the root we need to reconnect with – to remember and integrate – the unity of all beings, that no matter how different we may be we all have the right to be who we are. To hate implies a complete separation between self and other, as well as a level of self-obsession that denies any other reality.

Pride

This is the fourth of our hindrances. Immediately an image comes to mind of a cock, proudly strutting up and down a farmyard, displaying his colours for all to see! Pride is a sense of achievement that we have done something special, and often this feeling is necessary to enable us to go further. However, when it becomes competitive and moves into envy and jealousy then problems arise. Here again we are seeing the ego expressing itself through our separate accomplishments. In an egoless state we would be able to acknowledge our skills and achievements and be detached from owning them – they would simply be what they are without our need to be identified through them. When good or bad things happened we would not have to boast or complain about them, we would just see them in relation to all other things.

Jealousy and envy are further extensions of pride. Here our sense of separation causes us to think of others as better than us, prettier or richer, creating uncontrollable desire in ourselves and even hatred. This will continue until we are able to see that we all have something special and unique, that what another has is not better or worse than what we have. Whether we are rich or poor, we each have issues to work with, for power, wealth or beauty are not signs of inner freedom. A rose is beautiful and smells sweet. It does not ask us to smell it or get upset if we do not. It is simply a rose. Are we not as inherently beautiful and sweet as a rose? Can we not be who we are naturally, without jealousy or envy? If we can, as Yoko Ono says in *The Way Ahead*, transform our jealousy into admiration, then the pain will ease.

Doubt

The fifth hindrance is that of doubt, especially doubting truth. We have been given an enormously rich and powerful legacy in the form of the traditional teachings of all the religions and faiths that have been passed down over the centuries. These teachings have been tried and tested for thousands of years and there is little doubt that, even though they appear different – even contradictory – they can all ultimately direct us towards a state of freedom. They are not truth itself, for that is within us, but they can point the way to truth.

However, many of us have come to doubt the validity of such teachings. It is as if their very ancientness now makes them redundant, for human nature has surely become more sophisticated over the years and now we need new teachings to suit our modern mind. Or perhaps it is really because these teachings ask of us that we look at ourselves with honesty and humility. Rather than having to do this it is certainly easier to doubt and disbelieve! Unfortunately the traditional approaches have the drawback of appearing either so good and pure, or so rigid and formed, that they seem difficult to approach and relate to. Most of us feel we could never be that good or able to do what is being asked of us. We may become fearful of them, seeing them as a law that can punish us, or we reject them as absurd.

Being in a place of doubt can actually be very transformative as it can make us question everything we are doing. There is great validity in questioning the teachers and the teachings, as well as different belief systems. It means we are not taking anything as gospel without first asking if it is meaningful for us personally.

However, doubt also tends to pull us away to a safe and non-committed place, where we can watch without having to participate. Here no demands are made on us, we can maintain our illusions without being challenged. The opposite of doubt is trust. Without trust we get stuck in one place, unable to let things be as they are. Trust implies the ability to surrender control whereas doubt implies the need to hold on to control and power, so as to hold on to life as we know it.

False views

False views are the final hindrance and they are closely linked with the ignorance we spoke about above, for they are based on the ignorance of our true Self. For instance, the false view that we are solid and permanent will lead to great suffering, for there is nothing that is permanent, not a thought, a feeling or even a great mountain. We cling to permanence as a way of avoiding fear, the unknown and death. We cling to the content, but content is not the essence. If we are able to embrace impermanence we will find a greater beauty than we could have imagined, a beauty of movement, change and transformation.

There is also the false view that there is no such thing as cause and effect. In other words, this view believes that we can hurt or abuse someone else and not be hurt ourselves, can rob or steal and be able to walk away unaffected. It believes that we are all separate and not influenced by each other or by our own actions in any way. Yet when we see the law of cause and effect for what it is then we see how intricately inter-related all phenomena are, how totally dependent all things are on all other things.

Another false view is the belief that extremes such as idol-worship or asceticism have some great significance. Idol-worship could only be important if there were some form of external figurehead or god watching every move we make. The opposite, asceticism, would only have value if the body were some form of hindrance we have to deny in order to be free. Both are distorted visions of reality, as they fail to see that freedom lies within us, that it is our very nature, inherent to each one of us.

Meditation

One of the most traditional and well-practised methods of dealing with the ego and its many manifestations is through meditation. This is not necessarily the contemplation of an issue or problem, but rather the development of a completely calm state. When we practise sitting or walking meditation, allowing the mind to become quiet, receptive and still, we have the opportunity to go beyond the normal chatter that fills our days and creates all the chaos and fear in our minds. We have time to connect with the essence of all life, to find the true Self beyond the ego. Here we can develop an inner awareness of the mind as it really is, beneath the superficiality.

We can start by simply observing the mind and whatever arises within it. This gives us a chance to see the many tendencies of the mind and we learn to be more skilful by such observation. If we think of the mind as being like an ocean and our thoughts like the waves, then through observation the waves slowly become smaller. However, we cannot *make* the mind be still, that would be like trying to iron water! Instead we need to let the mind be in its own beingness so that the natural stillness within can be realized.

In the Buddhist teachings we find five basic mental hindrances that stop us from not only being able to meditate but from being able to look within ourselves at all. First, desire, beyond the fulfilment of our normal needs, especially for food, sex or other sensory delights, as these obviously distract us from achieving a calm and clear mind or from being free of attachment. Second, hatred or ill-will, which generates resentment, emotional imbalance, and creates such a strong disturbance that our mind becomes obsessed. Third, doubt, the lack of faith or trust which stops us from being able to commit ourselves to the meditation practice itself. This is a basic inability to recognize the importance of our higher consciousness. Fourth, sloth or torpor, whic:. is a mental dullness and lack of energy, draining us of desire to practise or to be mindful. Fifth, restlessness or anxiety which keeps us on edge, worrying and fretful, anxious and unable to stay still or be focused. It distracts us from being present.

There is a wonderful description of these states in *Human Enlightenment* by Sangharakshita, where he describes how the mind that is full of desire is like water to which many bright colours have been added. This makes the water very pretty, but the original purity and clarity of the water has gone. The mind that is distracted by hatred is like water that is boiling hot, hissing and bubbling. The mind that is full of doubt is like water full of mud, thick and unclear. The mind that is weakened by sloth and torpor is like water which has so many thick weeds in it that nothing can get through them. The mind distracted by restlessness and anxiety is like water whipped up into great waves by a strong wind. Finally, the mind that can overcome these hindrances becomes completely clear and calm, like a high mountain lake on a summer's day.

Who am I?

We have already discussed how the primary difficulty that arises in dealing with the ego is the deluded thinking that we are all separate from each other and how this delusion is what normally dominates our daily existence. In the last chapter we also looked at the twelve links of conditioned co-dependence that surround the Wheel of Life. These show how such a belief in separation has no validity as one state of existence arises always dependent upon the one before it, no condition or state of being can arise independently. Each and every form of life, every breath, thought and feeling, arises due to its dependence on something else. An unknown author wrote,

> All things by immortal power are
> To one another joined
> So that one cannot disturb a flower
> Without the troubling of a star.

We are all completely and intricately linked. Yet we identify so strongly with the content as being who we are – we cling to our thoughts, opinions, actions – that we forget we are not the thoughts, are not the opinions.

However, if we are not separate beings with independent existence, then who are we? Let us take a minute to try to find out who we are, what we mean by 'I' or 'me'. Do we mean our arms, our legs? Our vision, our senses? Or perhaps our personality? As Khentin Tai Situpa observes,

> Of course if someone asks, 'Who are you?' we will tell them our name. But if we really investigate from the outside inward, layer by layer through every part of our body until we reach the heart, we will never find the 'I' as a solid thing to which we can point and

say, 'This is me'. Then, since we are not sure that 'I' exists, and now that we have discovered that it is not physical, we have to investigate time and space to find it.

Eventually we discover that time and space are not solid either. In fact we begin to see that there is actually nothing solid, nothing we can call 'me' that exists independently of anything else. His Holiness the Dalai Lama adds to this understanding in his book *Kindness, Clarity and Insight*, where he says,

> The I appears from within the context of the mind and body; however if you investigate these places from which it appears, you cannot find it. Similarly, with regard to this which we point out as a table, if you ... investigate its nature, searching among its various parts and separating out all of its qualities, there is no table left to be found as the substrate of these parts and qualities.

We cannot say it is the 'I' that did this or that, as the past no longer exists, yet nor does the future, so where are we? Where do we find this special 'I' that we are so busy clinging to? Is it our mind? Is that what constitutes 'I'? Maybe it is, but if we penetrate the fabric of the mind, do we find anything real or permanent? Is it not that who we are – who we all are – is that which is completely and always will be free? We forget that the content is not the essence, and that the essence in each one of us is the same.

Finally we recognize that this is the true meaning of the haunting ghost – the realization that the ego is like a ghost because it actually has no substance, no solid reality that we can call its own. When we go searching for it, it is nowhere to be found.

Perhaps we can now begin to see how illusory the ego is, creating this wonderful image of ourselves that actually does not exist! Father Thomas Keating, in an essay entitled 'The Search For The Ultimate Reality', talks about when Lazarus fell seriously ill but Jesus did not come to heal him.

> What is the nature of this mysterious illness that came upon friends of Jesus and which he refused to heal? It is the recognition of one's false self and the sense of spiritual poverty that results from this awareness. The false self might be described as the

constellation of all the self-serving habits that have been woven into our personality from the time we were conceived . . . The story of Lazarus is . . . the teaching that one has to lose one's life in order to save it: to lose one's false self in order to find one's true Self . . . The death of the false self is the necessary condition for inner resurrection.

In other words, the image we have of the false self means we live in a dream, a fabricated structure that has no basis in reality. Every attempt at solidity and permanence is found to be unable to sustain itself, when all the trappings are taken away there is nothing but a vast emptiness. Finally we are left with that which transcends all phenomena, our true Self. However – luckily for us – this emptiness, this true Self, is the most beautiful, rich and abundant emptiness we could possibly imagine!

3

The Sacred Myth of Freedom

As we search for meaning and understanding in our lives we often encounter variations on the theme of self-responsibility. Yet the thought of taking responsibility for ourselves easily appears somewhat daunting. Being responsible seems like a burden weighted down by thoughts of duty and morality. We would much rather think of being free, spontaneous, not having to answer to anyone. But the word 'responsibility' can translate as the 'ability to respond', and in particular to respond to ourselves. Thus responsibility may actually become liberating in itself rather than burdensome. Responding to ourselves implies listening to and really hearing what we are feeling inside, honouring our own insight with the respect it is worthy of, trusting what we find as being real and valid. We become response-able to ourselves, to others, and thus to our world as a whole.

However, many of us were raised by being shouted at, made to feel insecure and uncertain, told that adults know best or that our feelings were not relevant. 'Children should be seen but not heard.' Few of us were given the acknowledgement that our opinions were equally as important as everyone else's. To trust in our own judgements and feelings is therefore quite hard, let alone to feel responsible for them. The universe does not always seem like a very friendly place. Therefore, we tend to turn outside of ourselves for validation and answers, to look for some form of authority to give meaning and direction to our lives.

We turn to the Church, temple or mosque, to a guru, to a teacher, a therapist, or to a specific technique, in the belief that this will take away our problems, will heal us, answer our questions, make us better people or our lives actually worth living. We pray to 'God' without any clear idea of who or what God is, other than as some form or something beyond ourselves that can dissolve our doubts and confusions and tell us what we are meant to do. We make others responsible for our happiness and then blame them for our unhappiness. When things go well we thank God; when they go badly we chastise ourselves, convinced that God has failed us or we are being punished. The belief that something separate and external can save us has the effect of forming a cage around us. And even though we are inside, we believe that the cage represents freedom.

By projecting our search outwards we do not have to deal with the reality of our inner chaos. We are told that as long as we practise something enough – whether it be prayer, mantra recitation, hatha yoga, atonement, meditation – we will become free of our limitations, maybe even enlightened. The external figure, technique or practice then becomes a symbol for our peace of mind and our freedom. It is not as if the practice itself is wrong – there is no doubt that prayer or meditation are essential components of the spiritual path – but they are the means not the end.

The Sacred Myth of Freedom

In holding on to this belief that freedom lies in something outside of us we actually make this something very sacred. But by making it sacred it immediately becomes limited and bound by our expectations. For instance, some years ago, when Eddie was spending time at a meditation centre, he noticed one of the women arranging some beautiful flowers on a table by the chair of the teacher who was due to speak later that day. Eddie went to smell the flowers, only to be told by the woman, 'Oh, no, you cannot smell them until guru smells them first!' It was a wonderful example of something becoming so sacred that it went beyond the bounds of rationality! However, a few years later that same woman, who had appeared to be such a devout follower, heard a story about the guru that upset her. Almost immediately she condemned him. She had put him on such a precious and godlike pedestal that she could not reconcile the sacred image she had created with the real one that showed he was simply human.

We long for the sacred to be a part of our lives, but in projecting our limitations upon an external image of freedom it loses its original genuineness and meaning. We then become very proud of our own idea of what freedom means, even if that includes being prejudiced against another's idea of freedom. Thus we bring the sacred down to the level of the mundane. For instance, freedom to the Ku Klux Klan is getting rid of the blacks – by getting rid of something we do not have to face it in ourselves. Freedom to an evangelical Christian is getting rid of all other religions, for surely they represent paganism and the anti-Christ? Freedom to a fighter in a Holy War (such as in the Middle East) means dying in battle so as to become a saint in the hereafter. Freedom to someone else will be having a sports car or being able to jet to Hawaii!

There is also the myth that freedom lies somewhere in the future, somewhere ahead of us. We believe that once we have done this or achieved that, then we can be free – if we are good then we will go to heaven. But until this particular thing is accomplished we have to suffer, be bound down, it is our lot we have to bear. It may be seen in a mother who cannot be free until her children are happy, or an aspiring business person who cannot feel worthy until he or she has achieved success. We do not realize that by changing ourselves we can change our world, rather than having to wait for the world to change first. Sadly, as soon as this first obstacle is out of the way and freedom is therefore looming close, another obstacle immediately comes along to delay freedom once more! For is not facing freedom the biggest obstacle of all?

This is therefore the sacred myth: that what we get, do, or believe in will give us freedom. As we are convinced that being free also means being happy, so happiness and freedom therefore appear inter-dependent, we cannot have one without the other. As our happiness is usually dependent on external circumstances, so also is our freedom.

Yet we only have to look at examples such as some of the Tibetan refugee prisoners – held in jail by the Chinese for many years in the most atrocious of conditions, and who later emerged from their captivity in a state of inner peace and tranquillity – to see that the freedom we really need to be talking about is the freedom within us, regardless of circumstances, and not one that is dependent on external conditions. True freedom enables us to accept both good and bad events without identifying with either. By recognizing that the events themselves are simply reflections of duality (a separate you and me) and not of oneness (a united you and me) they lose their impact and we can remain calm and at peace.

Love Thy Neighbour

There have been numerous religious and holy wars throughout the ages, some of which continue nowadays. It is extraordinary to realize that one man's belief in his religion versus another's belief in their religion can result in a war. For did not all the great teachers urge us to 'Love thy neighbour as thy brother'? Where are the teachings that tell us that if another man's belief is different to our own then we should fight and even kill him? In the name of Christ, Mohammed and many other great masters we have seen so many lives lost.

In the Middle East a war was waged over a piece of land and a quantity of oil, another over what is called Holy land. Yet is not human life more holy? Have our priorities become so distorted that human life is cheap enough to just discard, yet land is so precious? Is money more sacred than life? Is greed the primary motivating factor in our human existence? And in reality is this a fight not with another religion but with ourselves, with our own shadow – that dark and denied part of ourselves that we project on to others and who we then try to annihilate – is it not a fight with that which threatens our security simply because it is different?

A similar conflict can be seen in the world of gurus and teachers. The image of a perfect being is projected on to the guru, one who cannot make mistakes or act out of accord. This projection is so strong that it enables us to accept all varieties of untoward behaviour, from sexual abuse to alcoholism or extreme materialism. Yet when the teacher behaves in a way that is not agreeable and finally the reality emerges that this person is actually just like us – just as vulnerable and human – then we lose faith.

The teacher is usually equated with the teaching, so if the teacher lets us down then we feel let down by the teachings as well and thus have no guidance to support us. Having projected a sacredness on to the teacher as the means for our salvation, we are confronted by our own limitations and become dispirited and confused. Can the teaching stand for itself if the teacher falls? The battle in our own minds creates endless scenarios, we lose perspective and point fingers. But who is really doing the pointing? Are we not being pointed back into ourselves?

This is a form of *conditional misery*, meaning that our state of happiness or misery becomes conditioned by and is dependent on the external object of our projection. We forget that the method, the religion or the teacher is only the raft, the boat, the means to get across, but is not the other shore. For instance, going to confession may indeed help us feel better about our actions, but in the long run our behaviour will bring its own results that we have to deal with and to which confession has made no difference. If we are able to recognize what we are doing, to forgive ourselves and integrate change, then a true absolvement can take place.

As we saw in the last chapter, our lives are dominated by a fear of emptiness, a fear of being confronted with ourselves and finding nothing there. This fear makes us create all sorts of 'isms' and belief structures – different forms of escape, ways through which we can validate the ego, avoid the emptiness and instead be filled with ritual, organization and dogma.

Religion

One of these is religion which influences and dominates nearly all of humankind. Its very existence is indicative of our need for involvement with the divine, with the sacred in our lives, as well as for some form of external teaching and guidance to steer us through life's uncertainties. However, religion has largely become a fixed and lifeless institution, fulfilling little of these needs. In place of the divine we find rules and forms and structure. If we do not follow these then we are warned we will fall into sacrilegious and sinful ways.

This is a long cry from the purity and inspiration of the

Religion

teachers who preceded the structure. It is interesting to note that the Buddha was not a Buddhist, Jesus was a Jew not a Christian, Mohammed was not a Muslim, and so on. These men were the wise ones of their time who urged us to look within ourselves and to develop unconditional love for all beings. They did not talk of themselves in any grand or elevated way, but rather in the humblest of terms. Jesus washed the feet of his disciples, the Buddha lived as a wandering monk in the forests – both expressions of natural humility, of oneness with God. These people did not teach us to be arrogant or selfish, to make their path greater than any other, or to fight wars in their names. It was the followers of such teachers that deified them, creating the shrines, images, buildings and organizations.

If we look at the original teachings of the great religions we certainly do find differences, but this variety can stimulate us to delve deeper into our own understanding, rather than being a cause for division. We also find many similarities. Throughout there is an emphasis on giving to and loving others, even beyond ourselves, as selfishness is seen as the root of suffering. The need for inward reflection is also stressed, as the means to experiencing the highest truth, beyond the level of mundane reality. Humankind's relationship to God varies in each tradition, from our being the child of the Father to recognizing the God within ourselves, but the similarity lies in the evidence of a higher power than we are normally in communication with.

Types of practice also differ from prayer or communion to silent meditation, but the object is the same: to become connected to this higher power in whatever form we may perceive it and to become one with our divine essence. As Father Thomas Keating says, 'Perhaps the most precious value that the world religions have in common is their accumulated experience of the spiritual journey. Centuries of seekers have discovered and lived its conditions, temptations, development and final integration.' For instance, in Buddhism it says that the Buddha nature is within each person, so when Buddhists prostrate to an image of the Buddha they are in fact prostrating to that which is within themselves – their own higher Self. In Judaism, children are told how God is invisible, but does this not really mean that God is in-visible, or visible within?

However, as we move from the original teachings to the modern-day expression of these teachings we find dramatic differences. From seeing God in every one we now only see God in our own faith and all other faiths are automatically heretic. From loving our neighbours we are now at war with them, guarding our own way of life and making it sacred, despite the injunction, 'Thou shall not kill.' No doubt if the enlightened teachers from the past were to come to earth they would not recognize the hate and prejudice that has evolved as having anything to do with their original teachings at all. Instead of experiencing the mystery of God-consciousness, we now attend church once a week, cross ourselves or prostrate at the sight of an icon or statue, absolve ourselves through confession, have to wear hats in order to pray, put ashes all over our bodies, or touch our heads to the ground five times a day at pre-ordained moments.

As Anne Bancroft points out in *The Spiritual Journey*, 'We cling to the ritual and religious form as some sort of authority . . . yet does the outward form express the inner love, life or experience of God? Is it not merely a way of distracting us enough that we do not question what we are doing?' Have we, therefore, made religion a confining structure, a business, rather than an experience of freedom and joy? Has organized religion become a form of spiritual materialism? Have we made the names and forms so sacred that in comparison we are not possibly worthy of such divinity?

The great masters taught so that we may be liberated from our confines, but through fear we have created even greater limitations, translating the teachings in an impersonal way so as to avoid personal confrontation. The teachings say we are all one, but we see the teacher as the only one, different and separate from us. To have a religious experience is to feel deeply the presence of that which is divine and pure love, to see the sacredness within ourselves and the forms for what they are. Yet those who do experience this are thought of as over-emotional, even blasphemous or crazy – in the old days they would have been burned at the stake – rather than as experiencing true religious intent.

Perhaps one of the most interesting differences in the religious teachings is that of sin, which literally means to 'miss the mark'. Thus sin is not merely to transgress in our behaviour, but is more of a failure to be focused in and at one with God. We are missing the mark by failing to be aware of God consciousness and our actions reflect this lack of awareness. In today's Christianity, however, we find that behavioral sin is considered to be universal, inevitable, and implies complete estrangement both from self and from other. Adam was the first to sin by eating the apple and none of us are allowed to forget the enormity of this act! As Huston Smith says of Adam in *The Religions of Man*, 'As his sin was directly squared against God, it was of infinite proportions. Sins must be compensated for, otherwise God's justice is outraged. An infinite sin demands infinite recompense, and this could only be affected by God's vicarious assumption of our guilt.'

We can see some humour in this, for surely if God did not want Adam to eat the apple he would not have taken Adam to the tree, pointed at it, and told him not to eat it? However, our sins normally alienate us from humour, joy and participation in life, we become tense, isolated and lonely. Our sins cause us to become separated from others – as well as from God – and therefore from our true nature.

This idea of perpetual sin is only relieved by *atonement*. In its essence, atonement is a reconnecting with God as it is the re-establishing of our at-one-ment. We can, at last, reconnect with our oneness with all life. However, in modern-day practice we see atonement being used not so much to become one with God, but simply to excuse wrong behaviour and give us licence to do it again. It means we can avoid taking full responsibility for our actions; instead we leave that responsibility with God, presuming that this all-encompassing Father has time to deal with all of the guilt and avarice that we heap upon his shoulders! In this way only God is good, while the rest of us are mortal sinners.

In Buddhism, as another example, we find quite a different attitude towards sin. Here there is no right or wrong, no good or bad, simply skilful and unskilful. This implies that we can learn from our actions, take responsibility for them and personally deal with the results of those actions that cause harm or pain. Unskilful acts are hurtful, bringing sadness, confusion and mistrust; they are acts associated with greed, hatred and delusion. These acts turn us away from the truth, blinding our faith and spirit. In performing such acts we suffer the consequences, if not immediately then at some future time, for we cannot harm another without harming ourselves in some way. But rather than becoming alienated through such acts and having to be punished for them, instead we are directed to recognize the nature of the deed as being unskilful and to respond accordingly.

Skilful actions are ones that are generous, kind, selfless, compassionate and sensitive, bringing joy, comfort and safety; they are associated with contentment, warmth and wisdom. They are acts that enable others to grow in awareness, increasing their understanding of truth, thus assisting them to become more skilful themselves. As we develop in skilfulness we can purify the unskilful elements. Thus discovering our own peace is a skilful act as it means we are not expressing anger or hatred to the world.

By looking at just this one example, we can see how easily we become attached to our particular understanding and create the false or sacred belief that this is the only way. If the Christian is seeing humankind as being in a state of sin, then surely, in their eyes, Buddhists are sinning almost beyond recompense by their belief that they are the ones responsible for their actions and that God has nothing to do with it. And the ardent Buddhist, believing that sin is not a universal issue but a personal one – or that if there is sin at all then the greatest sin is ignorance as from ignorance arises all unskilful actions – thinks that confession and atonement are simply ways of avoiding the real issue. In truth, neither way is better than the other. They are simply different, appropriate for different people.

Perhaps one of the greatest hindrances that is encountered in trying to understand the separation of the religions is the basic level of insecurity from which humankind tends to operate. Generally speaking we are not free and independent thinkers; the majority of us follow set patterns in belief structures and behaviour models. This creates a sense of belonging, of being a part of the whole. The need to belong to a family/

group/clan is very instinctive. Participating in a group activity therefore fulfils this deep need and enables us to find a level of security and identity without which we can feel lost or alienated. Having found this identity, any opposition or questioning of it becomes a threat, a rocking of the boat. How can we open ourselves to understanding another way of being when we are so desperately clinging to our own way as a means of security?

Yet if we are closed to other religions and teachings, is it not because we suspect that maybe what they are saying could also be the truth? That if we listen we may find we do not have the only way to access God? But if we accept another way as being valid in itself, does that mean we are being converted to it? And if we are afraid of conversion, is it because we do not completely trust our own teachings as containing the truth?

If we look deep enough we may find that ultimately we need to discover our own path. However, it is a far more solitary journey to break away from traditional values and explore new ways of being than it is to stay within the confines of an organized structure. To follow our own path implies having the deep inner conviction that the truth is within. This conviction gives us the confidence to be open and receptive, to be able to hear all ways, not just one. When we can listen with our hearts to the various teachings that influence this world we may find they are not so threatening after all, that they actually have something to offer of real value. But if we listen with our heads then we will come up with all sorts of resistances and fears, we will be closed to learning anything new.

When we listen with our hearts then we discover that one of the common denominators to all religions is the emphasis that is placed on love. As His Holiness The Dalai Lama says in *Kindness, Clarity and Insight,*

> The development of love and compassion is basic, and I say this is the main message of religion . . . on that level there is hardly any difference between Buddhism, Christianity, or any other religion. All religions emphasize betterment, improving human beings, a sense of brotherhood, and sisterhood, love – these things are common.

We need to be reminded of this as it is love that enables us to come out of our heads and all the separatist concepts therein and to come into our hearts, to the place where we go beyond our differences and experience the essence of our similarities. Huston Smith says love is 'the only power that can quench the flames of fear, suspicion and prejudice, and provide the means by which the peoples of this great earth can become one to one another'.

This reminds us how Christianity was built upon the expression of love, seen particularly in the early Christians who felt so freed from their guilt, fear, and their separation from God, that they became infused with unconditional love. Through the love of Christ, these first followers become one with that love. In the Eastern religions we see this universal love being expressed through unswerving compassion for all living things. The Jains will even sweep the path in front of them so as to avoid stepping on or harming even the smallest of insects. They consider all beings to be equal with no boundaries or limitations between any.

However, even love can become prosaic and misused, reduced from its true essence of unconditionality to a personal and manipulated idiom. For as long as we believe that the religion, the teaching or the form itself is our route to salvation, then we will use whatever means of expression is appropriate to add further delusion. Ultimately the truth has to be found by and within ourselves. There is nothing to get and no one who can give it to us.

The myth of freedom is that someone else can act as an intermediary between ourselves and God, and thus the intermediary becomes sacred. In fact the truth – God – is already within us. It is simply our own limitations that bind us, the dust on the mirror that prevents us from seeing our true reflection, for are we not God's image in human form? Is it not possible that God made humankind in his image so that he would have playmates? But instead we started playing with each other and forgot about playing with God! Is the game not to find the God that is in each of us, or have we lost the ability to see creation as a play of God?

Gurus and Sects

Emerging out of a frustration and disillusionment in the Western world with traditional religion has come the age of gurus, their particular sects, and 'new' codes of behaviour. Many of these approaches are actually quite similar to the more traditional ones. For instance, they demand adherence to particular teachings and tend to imply that their path is the right one, if not the only one. They also encourage a group identity, the forming of a family, so that a sense of security is found within the group rather than outside it.

Gurus and Sects

There have been many gurus from the East that have come to the West in the last few decades, and there are some Westerners who have started their own groups. Because these new teachers have appeared fresh and alive compared to the inertia of the institutionalized Church, they have attracted large numbers of people who have long wanted the spiritual teachings to have more meaning in their lives.

Most of us were raised listening to sermons condemning our behaviour, living in fear of punishment from above, or kneeling on cold floors being told to pray to someone or something we had no real relationship with. The new gurus came with a joy and laughter we had not known before, teaching us how to find inner happiness, making us feel special and wanted. Joining such a group is like joining a family, finding a place for ourselves that had not felt available before; it is the discovery of new relationships with similar people – suddenly we are no longer alone. The good feelings also engender new spiritual intent, the teachings become real and meaningful, something that can be integrated into every aspect of our lives.

In particular the gurus encourage us to have a direct relationship with them, to take them into our hearts and to feel the aliveness of such a relationship. This provides the opportunity for us to have a personal and immediate contact with an aware and awakened being, something we may never have had before. God has always felt so far away, distant, authoritative, irrelevant to our daily lives. Now God is manifest in a form that is alive, touchable, graspable, and related to us personally. This is a tremendous inspiration, a direct experience that makes the possibility of our own awakening a real one.

It is the lineage of this student–teacher relationship that has kept the traditional teachings alive throughout the centuries, as such contact with an awakened being can stimulate our own understanding. In particular a good teacher has the ability to reflect back to us when we are being ego-centred – in guru jargon this is known as being busted! Thus the guru keeps us present and aware of our actions, constantly reminding us of our purpose and commitment to egolessness. As Ramana Maharshi says in *The Spiritual Teachings of Ramana Maharshi*, 'The guru is both external and internal. From the external he gives a push to the mind to turn inward; from the interior he pulls the mind toward the Self.'

Without such a teacher we can easily delude ourselves into thinking we have achieved a level of spiritual maturity when it may, in fact, just be spiritual materialism – the belief that we have gained spiritual understanding when in reality it is a solidifying of the ego. Rather than a letting go it is a gathering of more. The role of the guru is to help us to see the ego, to see ourselves clearly, it is not another means of avoiding ourselves.

A true guru is therefore a true friend. However, when we enter into such a relationship it is important to be very aware of what we are doing, even to be sceptical and to test the guru, until we are sure that we can be in a place of trust with this person. It is a trust on both sides – there should be as much love, compassion and respect from the teacher as there is from the student. There are inherent dangers whenever we allow another person to have any form of control or power over us, so any doubts or uncertainties we have should be respected. Too often we hear of conflicting incidents due to an unquestioning faith that is blind to what is really happening, or as a result of deifying the guru beyond the human level.

For, unfortunately, some of these new gurus have taken the personal relationship issue further than the God of our childhood prayers did! Stories of sexual abuse, promiscuity and the use of drugs and alcohol have abounded through the press. The transition from the traditional mode of guru and disciple that has been maintained for hundreds of years in the East to the far more liberal and uninhibited ways of the West, has created many difficulties. Gone are the usual parameters as Westerners are used to being very independent and outspoken compared to their more modest and humble Eastern brothers and sisters. The lure of Western luxury has also brought down many of those who at first were sincere teachers.

Some groups encourage the wearing of a particular colour or dress, or a picture of the teacher as it can be helpful in reminding the practitioner of their commitment. However, on the subtle level it can also encourage the followers to feel they are special, are in God's grace, implying that others are not. Perhaps the need for such an external expression does not always spring from a wholesome discarding of material attachments and an openness to the divine, but rather from a deep insecurity and fear of being lost and alone. It is also a way to hold the group together, to make it a cohesive unit without dissidents, to ensure continuation.

Expressing group identity through, for instance, each member wearing the same coloured clothing, has the effect of separating those who are 'in' versus those who are not. This can, inadvertently, lead to the development of cults, a move away from the original intent of discovering freedom. It is the development of 'gurudom' where too much emphasis is put on the physical manifestation instead of on the spiritual experience. For those gurus who fall prey to the lures of power, their actions become that of gurudom rather than guru, of being all-powerful while the student becomes powerless.

There are many teachers in this world who have been able to sustain their deep vision and understanding, such as Christ or Buddha. For others there may have been a great insight, a sudden flash of awareness, and this experience has encouraged them to teach and share their understanding. But unless the realization of truth permeates our every cell then we all, whether gurus or not, will be equally as susceptible to the lures of power, passion and greed. The teachings may well be true and valid, but living in the position of being loved over and above all others and having every word we utter immediately acted upon, easily gives rise to delusion. If we ourselves can fall, then can we not see how easily another may also do so?

However, the sadness lies not so much with the gurus who have gone astray, as it does with the many hundreds of devotees who have followed them, either into the abyss as with the well-publicized Jonestown episode (when Jim Jones led his followers into a mass suicide), or into a deeper sense of alienation and separation from others. In our need to find something sacred amidst the confusion of our normal reality we project on to the guru all our images of purity, godliness and specialness. The guru has to be different or nothing else has any meaning at all.

We forget that although the guru may have vast wisdom and compassion, he or she is still human – one does not contradict the other. Being in an awakened state does not exclude being ordinary. In fact, is it not our purpose to realize our ordinariness? But the follower who so projects the image of God on to the teacher, when confronted with ordinary humanness in this being, then either denies such mortality to be true, or loses all faith and belief in what he or she thinks of as spiritual or sacred.

Denial is usually the first stage. How can we accept a reality that implies the disintegration of our entire support system, maybe even of our homes, families and work? So much emphasis has been placed on the teacher as being someone special that when he or she no longer keeps their side of the arrangement then disbelief, abandonment and anger arise. The disbelief is enormous, but even more so is the feeling of being abandoned and let down. Rage and fury are common responses. It is easier to deny there is anything wrong for in denial we can maintain the illusion.

Our freedom lies in this other person staying sacred, we have been let down and have no idea how to cope with it. This is also because inherent within the devotion and worship of the guru is a tendency towards self-dislike, even self-denigration. How can we love ourselves with all of our neuroses and fears when we are seeing ourselves next to one as pure and perfect as the guru? Surely it is their light, not ours? We remember once commenting on how radiant a woman appeared and she modestly replied that it was not her light, it was the light of her guru. For in comparison we can only appear as insignificant and hopeless. Then if our image of the guru falls we are left confronting our own imperfections and become immersed in confusion and self-pity.

If there is an acceptance that the teacher has fallen from our ideals, then we tend to put the teachings in there too. How can we still believe in the teachings if the teacher was not practising them? If they led to such disgrace? There can be a tremendous emptiness that follows such an experience as life seems to have lost all direction and meaning, there is nothing real or dependable. We have been let down in the same old way, it wasn't God incarnate after all. What's the point in believing anything if it's all going to end this way eventually? We are confronted with our belief in the myth that something out there is more sacred than we are and will save us by granting us our freedom, and the realization that it cannot.

There can also be a feeling of having been deceived by the guru, or even of having deceived ourselves. This can lead to recalling other incidents where we felt that the guru had not acted appropriately but we had accepted such action because we believed the guru was closer to God and therefore knew more than we did.

To heal ourselves we have to acknowledge that the guru is within each one of us: to thine own self be true! Both of us have been through the traditional Indian training with a guru and know that there is tremendous value in this. However, realizing God is up to each one of us for ourselves, no one can do this for us. When we discover the guru within us, by listening to our own conscience, then we also discover that we are all equal – whether we are a teacher or a student – we are all on the same journey. This is a truly empowering realization.

We experienced this first-hand when we met with His Holiness The Dalai Lama in India. In seeing him, Debbie began to prostrate as this is the normal greeting. However, he made her stand up, saying, 'We are all equal here.' His casualness, simplicity and honesty as he sat with us and held our hands was such a relief. We had both met with many gurus before, but seeing the true humility in someone like the Dalai Lama was very reassuring. He is a living example of how being ordinary is genuine and truly liberating!

To be truly human is divine. Understanding that the guru is human, even ordinary, allows us to be less idealistic and more direct. Seeing simple, loving, human qualities in a being is rare and provocative. Gurus such as this are true treasures as they enable us to see the truth in ourselves, rather than seeing ourselves only in comparison. For how can we love God but not love ourselves – are they not the same thing?

The New Age

Parallel to the gurus and sects phenomena has been the emergence of what is commonly called the New Age, a title that has often been misunderstood. The New Age originated many years ago as a movement to bring about more humane approaches to our educational system, reform programmes, the environment and politics; it wanted to implement a change that would accommodate the fact that we are humans with feelings that should be respected rather than exploited, that we do not have to destroy each other or the planet in our desire to live here.

The New Age

However, over the years the New Age has developed quite a medley of ideas and the title now tends to cover a vast array of practices and beliefs, from crystal therapy to the tarot, psychic readings, colour healing, channelling, past life regression, astrology, soul travelling, dream analysis, and so on. The list is endless and often misleading. Unfortunately, in the mind of the general public, many traditional religious paths have also become associated with and thought of in this way, when in fact they are quite different.

The New Age definition is therefore somewhat vague and undefined with anything that speaks of being for one's growth and unfoldment generally getting put into this category. The varied subjects under this heading do tend to have one important thing in common, however, and that is the belief that we are here on earth to experience more than just a life of endless desire, vacillating between pleasure, pain and suffering, that we can grow beyond our limitations and experience a deeper joy, a greater wisdom and freedom. This is our natural birthright.

Added to this, many of the New Age teachings also stress that we can create what we want, whether it be vibrant health, abundant wealth, enlightenment, or the ideal partner. The choice is up to us, dependent upon how much we are prepared to let go of our old limited ways of being and become aware and awake to other possibilities. To help us there are numerous methods and techniques, some of which are perfectly valid in themselves while others may have less meaning or value.

Coming from a world of needing and not getting, of feeling restricted by circumstances, of right and wrong, of feeling tied by conventionality and set patterns, the New Age can offer a wonderful experience of expansion, openness and potential. It gives us the opportunity to go beyond the rational mind to see that anything is possible. It makes us look at who we are in relation to the whole, and allows us to break down our limitations in a safe environment. It also offers comradeship and family, a coming together that we may never have experienced before.

However, the emphasis in this environment is largely on 'me', on 'I want, I need, I feel, I think. . . '. This self-obsession may be necessary as we emerge out of our conditioned state, but it does not lead to true spirituality. Such an emphasis on the 'I' maintains the illusion of separation, of duality, and to reach any real, meaningful sense of connectedness and unity we have to go beyond the 'I'. The New Age can be very good at bringing us to this point, but can sometimes fall short in offering a path to the true freedom of egolessness. We do not, for instance, often hear words such as humility, generosity, selflessness or compassion, but rather ones such as abundance, achievement, power and personal need.

A further aspect that is emphasized is that of having positive emotions, or the expression of good and loving feelings towards all, even though this may be at the expense of being honest and straightforward with what we are *really* feeling! Although being loving is certainly far more preferable than being aggressive, there is not always enough room for expressing depression, fear or anger, for these are thought of as negative and destructive emotions. To have such negative thoughts is seen as blocking the flow of our fulfilment. Not wanting to be considered a failure, these feelings tend to get held back and repressed. This hinders any real release and resolution – there is an artificial brightness rather than a genuine mix of dark and light. For true development the descent into the pain and grief within us is equally as important as the ascent into the love and acceptance. In the New Age environment, however, the descent tends to be ignored in favour of the ascent.

The New Age also expresses the need for us to take responsibility for ourselves, but often does so in such a way that it can generate enormous guilt if we are seen not to! For instance, 'What have I done to attract this to me?' or 'What have I done to deserve such misfortune?' are typical thought patterns. These focus on the responsibility we should have to all things, but they can also hide a feeling of not being good enough, of a hopelessness and insecurity. They still emphasize the 'me'. It is easy to get caught up in trying to find a meaning for everything that happens, rather than simply seeing and acknowledging things for what they are without needing to personally identify with them. Perhaps it is not a matter of 'deserving such misfortune' as it is simply the fact that life is impermanent and all things change, no matter how hard we try to stop them!

The difficulty with all of these teachings lies yet again in drawing us outside of ourselves towards something or someone that appears to know better than we do and will give us the answers we seek. The ability to look within – to trust our own intuition and judgement, to be honest with who we are – is overshadowed by comparisons to and a longing to be like, for instance, the glamorous, loving or beautiful group leader. We are giving our power to someone else, rather than turning it towards ourselves.

Channelling

One of the more popular ways in which we do this is by going to the ever-growing number of channels or mediums. Where there used to be only a very few of these, scattered around the world, there now seems to be an abundance in every town, each channelling a spirit or disincarnate being, generally known by a medieval or foreign name! Let us not be misunderstood – it is possible that these people are very genuine in their message. However, we do not have any true criteria through which to judge the entities, there is no way of knowing if they are really respectable or are the mischievous ones wanting attention!

And are we even talking about disincarnate beings here, or an aspect of ourselves that we have made discarnate? Is it not possible that, due to a lack of self-worth and self-confidence, we are unable to accept our own wisdom and insight and so find a more acceptable and even exciting means to express ourselves and thus be heard? For so often we hear channels saying how they are the ignorant ones who do not know anything, while the entity is the one with all the wisdom and great insight. Yet in so doing, are we not ignoring that supreme intelligence that is inherent within each one of us, that is our true Self?

However, the difficulty here is not so much with the delusion or not of the actual channels, but with the sacred myth of freedom that surrounds them and the teachings. As with gurus, channels tend to attract large numbers of people and can have great influence over their lives. Whether it be advising a marriage, a divorce, foreseeing a change in job, predicting a move or some action in the future, or expounding on spiritual theories, the devotion is to each and every word. And, as with gurus, there is tremendous importance placed on the personal relationship – the fact that we are individually receiving attention and acknowledgement is extremely stimulating. Having received such benefit, we may even follow and revere the entity wherever he or she goes.

In our longing to be told what to do, we therefore face the same dilemma of off-loading responsibility for our decisions and actions on to someone else, believing that by living out their instructions we will become free. Yet are their instructions for us? Is what we are being told really appropriate for us at this time? Or are we following it out of a deep need for guidance, regardless of what that guidance might be and even if it is not right? Are we trying to fill the void with the hope that someone can give us? We tend to hold on to every word as if the word itself were direct from God and had a profound message just for us, that God is talking to us personally. It is very easy to deny our own intuition and understanding in this way. It is also true that real freedom actually means not holding on to anything, whether it be God's words or not!

One of the difficulties is that channelling and other similar activities are on the higher mental or psychic plane and this encourages a sense of psychic entertainment. There is a misunderstanding that takes place here as there is a tendency within the New Age to get caught up in this psychic realm and to see it as greater than it really is. When this happens then something such as the ability to channel is seen as the goal, as the purpose and reward for all our efforts, rather than simply being a step along the way. In many of the more traditional teachings we find references to psychic phenomena, psychic powers or mediumship, but we also find clear warnings not to get involved with such powers. To do so creates a distraction and delusion, making us believe we are something special and different because we appear capable of such feats. It thus becomes an ego booster, a detour leading us away from simplicity, humility and true spirituality to a place of glamour and personal power.

To go beyond the realm of psychic phenomena means to go deeper within ourselves. It means having the courage, the faith and the trust in our own wisdom; to be striving for spiritual depths rather than temporal ones. To go deeper also means being able to embrace and accept what we find within, such as our neurosis and confusion, and to work with this in a way that brings resolution. It is through insight and self-enquiry that we discover the wealth that is our real nature. Going deeper means being able to see through the ego to egolessness. Instead of being self-centred or self-indulgent, it is self-surrender. It is a giving, not a getting.

There may well be times when we need guidance, but when we are with a teacher we can apply the teachings within ourselves without having to glorify or deify the person. For the teachers are there simply to guide, not to be better than us, to take over or control. Awakening can only come through our own efforts, by and in ourselves.

Therapy

Since the turn of the century we have also seen an explosion in the therapeutic and psychological fields, giving rise to numerous different forms of therapy and counselling. In the last twenty years it has been considered fashionable to have a therapist, to be undergoing analysis, even to have to check our actions or decisions with our therapist first in case we make a detrimental move! In this way, therapists have replaced God, becoming associated with a means to freedom. This is despite the fact that the therapist may be just as confused as the one seeking therapy!

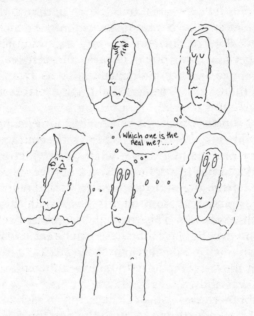

Therapy – Looking for the Real 'Me'!

Perhaps this glorification is not so surprising considering the deeply personal one-on-one relationship we have with a therapist. As we saw earlier, many of us are craving such recognition and find an answer through either becoming dogmatic and closed to other paths, by following a guru or channel, or by joining in the New Age seminar circuit. Being in therapy is another means we use to feel potent and important. At the same time, let us not undermine the valuable work that therapy does, often empowering us enough through difficulties

that we are eventually able to find the answers for ourselves. There are many times in our lives when we encounter
the monsters within and feel unable to cope, unable to find
our way through. When this happens then a good therapist or
counsellor can be invaluable, enabling us to find our way out
of the mire.

The drawback lies in becoming dependent on such a guide,
thus disempowering ourselves even further. We need to be
able to use the information and insight that is generated and to
move on from the therapist to our own understanding. However, the tendency is to become locked into the therapy mode
and to lose sight of our own purpose and wisdom, to forget
that we can stand on our own feet, and instead to put the
therapist above and beyond ourselves.

Within therapy the emphasis is usually placed on the ego,
the 'I', and with developing a strong sense of self and self-
identity to replace the chaos and confusion. We are searching
for the real me, going through all the different aspects of our
personality in a bid to discover who we are. Like the Russian
matryoshka or nesting dolls, we work our way through layer
after layer, from the outer persona to the more hidden inner
issues. This process is essential, but it can equally lead us into
further self-obsession. The 'poor me' syndrome is one we are
all familiar with, but in therapy this can be exaggerated until it
becomes an over-indulgence in ourselves.

Yes, it is important to heal the child within, to heal that part
of us that was abused, beaten down, ignored or denied. Without a doubt there are deeper conflicts within each of us and we
need to have the fortitude to bring these to the surface and to
accept them. But let us also have the ability to rise up from our
mud, from our darkness, and to head for the light, lest we
become immersed in the mud! Let us be able to accept and
even embrace those issues so full of pain within us, for when
we bring love to pain it can be healed. The monsters are only
fearsome when they are hidden in the shadows – brought into
the light they can be seen for what they are.

Drugs and Alcohol

During the 1960s we saw an explosion in the use of drugs, something that many found to be a joyful ecstasy giving a sense of great liberation, while others were terrified by the idea of being out of control. There is no doubt that with drugs it is possible to enter into altered states of consciousness and experience those parts of our minds with which we are usually out of touch. In this way many people had visions – glimpses of freedom, of spiritual insight – creating the possibility that there was something else, something more than our normal mind could perceive, and that we were capable of reaching these higher states of consciousness. For instance, LSD became an agent for personal change as users found themselves seeing into another reality, another dimension and way of being . It has been said that no one who has done an LSD trip has been left unchanged by it!

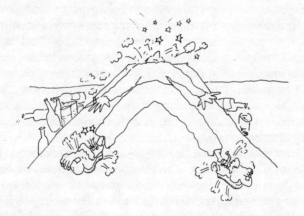

Drugs and Alcohol

However, this experience may not be a permanent one, for the user can later forget; the experience is dependent on ingesting the drug rather than on a natural opening of the mind through our own efforts. So although drugs may release us from the confines of the limited or conditioned mind, the result can create an illusion. They show us the top of the mountain but not how to get there! During the experience we believe we are free, beautiful, able to do anything we want, then we 'come down' and have to face the fact that we are just as confused as before. Hence there have even been some 'casualties', people who could not deal with ordinary reality in comparison to what they were experiencing on drugs and became mentally deluded, experiencing hallucinations even when not partaking.

Drugs have often been a starting point for beginning on the spiritual path, a catalyst creating a stimulus for us to search for those higher states from which our own understanding then emerges. If our understanding is genuine we will be able to see that the experiences and the freedom we long for are within us, and that they are available without our having to take anything.

Alcohol has been a problem for much longer and has generally been ignored more than drugs. It does not help us to reach higher states of consciousness as drugs may do, but it can certainly serve to obliterate the often unpalatable reality confronting us. We therefore begin to rely on it so that we do not have to deal with what is really going on. With alcohol we can build a cocoon, one that enables us to escape to a different place. It creates a distorted picture of the difficulties or tensions in our lives, in particular it hinders any true communication from taking place. How easy it is to have a drink and let the problems of the day drift away, especially since alcohol is so socially acceptable. Thus it has become one of society's more prevalent obsessions.

Addictions as a whole are a wonderful example of the sacred myth of freedom, the blind belief that we are actually free to do whatever we want when in fact we are just acting as a slave to our endless desires. In lacking the ability to find fulfilment within ourselves we try to find it in something outside of us – when the emptiness, meaninglessness and hopelessness of life become too much to bear it is like a deep hole needing to be filled up. We then use whatever means we can to fill this hole, whether it be food, drugs, sex, or even an addiction to doing all sorts of seminars!

Addiction is about our relationship to ourselves, of resentment and anger at the world for not fulfilling our desires, of not having a loving relationship with ourselves as we are. The addiction itself is to maintaining the neurotic and selfish aspects of the ego, regardless of the form this takes. As Debbie wrote in *The Bodymind Workbook*,

> We are all addicted in one way or another, and this addiction is to the preservation of our ego. Some people manifest this addiction – and all the fears and neuroses it brings with it – in an external way through addiction to something tangible; while others internalize it and become afraid of the dark or of being attacked.

However, the more we are able see how our addiction hurts us and is not in our best interests, when we can look at it head on, then the smaller the hole inside us will get!

Spiritual Egotism

There is a wonderful new phrase that has developed in the last few years, that of 'spiritual materialism', which implies all the spiritual practices, accomplishments, teachers and techniques that we have accrued, but which we have become possessive and attached to. Chogyam Trungpa says in *The Myth of Freedom*,

> If one searches for a promised land, a Treasure Island, then the search only leads to more pain. We cannot reach such islands, we cannot attain enlightenment in such a manner. . . . As long as one's approach to spirituality is based upon enriching ego, then it is spiritual materialism, a suicidal process rather than a creative one.

Spiritual Egotism

Out of spiritual materialism has arisen the 'spiritual ego', a form of ego that is possibly more damaging than a regular ego as it is suffering the delusion of delusions! Here we become so attached to our own progress – the ability to sit in meditation for hours at a time, or to be able to do the most complicated of hatha yoga postures – that we lose sight of the true purpose of our practice, which is that of becoming free. We may shave our heads, wear robes, take a spiritual name and begin to think we are somebody important. The belief then grows that this accomplishment is itself freedom, when in fact it is yet another form of bondage that the mind is holding on to. The need to be special, more advanced or better than others is so ingrained in our culture that we carry it along with us, like luggage, even on our spiritual journey.

In this way we conceptualize in order to avoid confrontation. There is a desire for freedom without actually wanting to change our basic nature; a pardoning of our sins without taking responsibility for them. We convince ourselves that we are following the path, doing all the right things, taking the right classes, practising faithfully every day, but beneath it all we are simply fortifying our egotistic image of ourselves. We stop being able to learn or to have an open mind for surely we already know the right way and the right answers so how can anyone teach us anything new? But again we have forgotten humility, simplicity, graciousness and gratitude.

Father Thomas Keating says in *The Way Ahead*,

> As one journeys across the desert, prairie or sea – images in sacred literature of the tedium of daily life – one may come upon a place of rest: an oasis, a garden of spiritual delights, or a harbour . . . It seems as if one has arrived at the end of a laborious journey and that one's immense efforts are at last coming to fruition. Actually, unless one hastens to push on, the place of rest becomes a place of poison. Spiritual consolation is a trap when sought for one's own satisfaction.

The delusion that comes in the way between the ego and true freedom is that there is an actual 'I' doing the achieving, an 'I' that is gaining spiritual knowledge. This delusion is due to the need for self-identity and personal power, yet it is also combined with a genuine desire for God realization.

This is another aspect of the consciousness of the third chakra that we talked about in the last chapter. This level is indeed the source of manipulation and ego: however, such consciousness can also lead us to the development of the fourth chakra energy, which is the opening of the heart. For from self-fulfilment and self-gratification can come the realization that these alone are not enough. The desire to serve, to discover a genuineness and realness to life that we have not found before, begins to arise. In other words, all the various means or methods that we choose to use do have great value if they can be seen as the raft, not the other shore. For no one technique will be able to open our hearts, no matter how long and hard we practise. That opening can only come from within, due to our motivation and willingness to let go of our attachments. As long as we recognize that true freedom is our inherent birthright, and that the teachings and the techniques are there just to guide us – not to possess us or for us to possess them – then we will find our way. The desire to give, not just to get, begins the awakening.

When the teachings become a living reality then there is no more achievement, nor even a goal to be reached, for there is no thought of self doing the achieving. We simply are. As Shunryu Suzuki says in *Zen Mind, Beginner's Mind*,

> In the beginner's mind there is no thought, 'I have attained something.' All self-centred thoughts limit our vast mind. When we have no thought of achievement, no thought of self, we are true beginners. Then we can really learn something. The beginner's mind is the mind of compassion. When our mind is compassionate it is boundless . . . We must have beginner's mind, free from possessing anything, a mind that knows everything is in change. Nothing exists but momentarily in its present form and colour. One thing flows into another and cannot be grasped.

From discovering the ego, to developing a spiritual ego, we can now become like beginners again, open and receptive, in touch with the natural laws of life rather than needing to be in control of them. For did Jesus not say that to enter the kingdom of God we should become like children?

4

Out of the Mind and into the Heart

Have we by now had enough of pain and suffering, of dualities and separation, of gratification without satisfaction? Have we begun to ask if there is not something more than this endless cycle of desire, accumulation, gain and loss? We have read the books and heard the teachings yet are we still caught up in the mind? Despite knowing that the mind is habitual, neurotic and even groundless, do we continue to believe our issues are solid – do the dramas play out over and again? Or have we finally got the message that all of this is an illusion, is not real? That to be living inside our heads all the time is actually not much fun? Have we fully grasped the fact that there is a place we can function from that is not subject to such chaos or limited by pain, fear and neuroses, but is actually joyful, creative, meaningful and loving?

When we reach such a point of dissatisfaction and questioning, when we have had our fill of suffering, then a shift can begin to take place. It is a shift of emphasis. From being locked into the head with all its attendant fears and manifestations, we become aware that there is this other part of our being that operates in a different way and is actually a source of great richness, only this wealth is one that cannot be squandered or lost. We realize that if we can come out of the endlessly distracted and discursive mind and into the heart, then we may find a real ease, a deep happiness awaiting us that previously we had never realized existed. This heart goes deeper than just the physical one. It is the core, the essence of

Out of the Mind and into the Heart

our being, a place of supreme love and compassion that lies within us all.

We can experience this open heart when walking along a beach, or through a wooded hillside, in a garden, watching a sunset, or when listening to music. It is a time when we seem to dissolve and the confusion or pain no longer dominates. Tears may spontaneously come to our eyes and there is a sensation of warmth and complete surrender. It is the letting go of fear and the need to control. As this happens, the heart opens and true love is experienced.

The awareness of this inner heart can also happen at a time when we are vulnerable and in a state of sadness, depression, loneliness, loss, grief or shock. It may be as a result of great trauma, such as severe illness or perhaps the death of a loved one, and we are faced with the meaningless and emptiness of life. The shift from head to heart is not always an easy transition. But when we are in such a state of tenderness and vulnerability we become open to other possibilities, there is accessed a more sensitive level of awareness.

We have heard stories of deep loss, of pain and abuse, states that so many of us experience. Yet through the difficult times we can develop an inner strength, determination, and a connectedness with love and compassion. We have personally witnessed the openness and heart-centred courage that can emerge from such ordeals, from the man who had polio who now teaches acting, to the victim of multiple incest who has found forgiveness for her abusers.

Debbie realized an open heart most profoundly when confronted with a near-death experience and the instant connection with the essence of all life – love – in that moment. 'Flying from New York to Dallas late at night, the small plane I was on suddenly caught the tail end of a tornado and was swung around like a feather in the sky. Having accepted that I was probably going to die and able to feel OK about that, I then realized that, in dying, I would not be able to tell the people I loved how I felt about them. The power of love filled my consciousness – a depth and magnitude I had never known before. In the weeks that followed I found myself merging with and living in an experience of love that both encompasses all life, all things, and at the same time is the very core and essence of life.'

Eddie's mother died five days after he was born and he was raised by his mother's elder sister. 'The Jewish family of six lived in a crowded apartment in the Bronx, New York. There was no personal space of any sort, so to find privacy there was nowhere to go but within oneself. As I matured the repressions I was surrounded by – the isolation and confines of the city – led me to search for a more sensitive way of being. One day I was on the Staten Island Ferry and, as the boat began to move away from the city and into the river, everything suddenly seemed to drop away. A deep feeling of universal love arose spontaneously. It was as if the movement of the ferry were symbolic for a letting go of resistance and fear.'

Each of us experiences such an opening of the heart in different ways. One friend had reached the age of 48 years old and yet he had never cried, never shed a single tear. He recalled how, just as he was experiencing a particularly frightening ordeal at school, he remembered his mother saying, 'Brave boys don't cry.' This had imprinted itself so deeply that his emotions had become blocked, held back, repressed. Now, through meditation and inner work, he was letting go of these long-repressed feelings. One day, as he came out of a deep relaxation, a single tear rolled down his cheek as he felt his heart come alive for the first time!

For another person it was quite different. Severely abused as a child she had later become an alcoholic. This led to a car crash in which she was paralyzed from the waist down. In recovery from the accident and from alcohol, she saw how the paralysis was connected to her unconscious desire to deny and even ignore what had happened to her sexually in the past – by numbing her body she was numbing her sexuality. She was able to heal only by realizing that the content is not the essence – that whatever may have happened to her was not who she was in essence. We tend to identify with our pain and with the events in our lives as being *us*, when in fact our essence, the real Self, is none of this. Through such an ordeal as this person had she saw that no matter what had happened, within her being she was free.

In such times of intense futility and hopelessness that can so engulf us there is this opportunity to connect with the openness and sensation of love that flows from within, a love that is love simply for its own sake, not directed to anyone in particular and with no selfish motives. It brings a deep abiding peace.

Why Are We Here?

It is not, by any means, a necessity that we go through a traumatic experience in order to open the heart, this shift of awareness can also arise spontaneously, without effort, like a flower opening, for it is our true nature. But the traumatic types of experience all have a similar quality. They confront us with a sense of futility, making us question why we are here, what the point of life really is. They make us wonder if this is all just a waste of time. Are we here only to live and die without anything else happening?

It is so easy to feel that nothing is worth while and to become depressed. Why do we go on walking the same tread-mill, going on and on without getting anywhere, facing the same loneliness or hopelessness day after day? Life does not always seem fair, for even if we have everything we could want we can still be miserable, and if we do not have every-thing then we tend to engross ourselves in trying to get it, thinking that in having there lies the answer to our complaints. We run after our happiness like a dog chasing its own tail, never quite being able to grasp it in our hands.

Some years ago Debbie started working in the psychiatric ward of a nursing home. 'Such a place can be instantly depressing. The inmates are not only old, but also mentally disturbed. One woman, who was strapped to her wheelchair, would do nothing all day long other than to rock back and forth moaning, 'Help me, help me, help me,' yet if anyone went to her aid she would recoil in terror. Within a few months I became ill – I had reached a level of despair, one in which the hopelessness of the human condition was overwhelming – and it was affecting me both physically and emotionally. If I saw teenagers or children walking towards me, I was seeing them not as teenagers but as old, decrepit and in need of help. Constantly I was asking myself what was the point in life? To go from a free and loving child to becoming useless and psychotic, needing to be strapped to a wheelchair? Why bother if this is all there is for us?

'Becoming ill helped me realize that I was losing touch with my heart. What I was seeing around me was the hopelessness and sadness of humankind, but I was forgetting that this need not be the only destiny awaiting us. I found my healing by reconnecting with the deeper purpose for our being here – that of becoming free of such neurotic states and finding a level of peace that takes us beyond our limited selves to an aware-ness of our true Self.

'This change was a profound and radical one. I realized I had become so involved that I had been taking on and experiencing the suffering of others as my own. Although my care and love for them was real it was leaving me wide open and therefore very vulnerable, allowing their pain and misery to enter into and affect my own life. What I had to do was develop the ability to be giving, loving and compassionate without identifying with the pain. I had to discover a detached compassion, a state where I could lovingly deal with the suffering without being emotionally affected by it.

'I saw I had to see beyond the situation to the truth of the person, without getting distracted by the suffering. For beneath the neurosis and fear in each one of us is our true and free Self. In relating to this I found I was able to give far more, was gentler and less critical, more patient and accepting. I was able to receive the suffering without taking it in, for I was relating to the essence inherent within each person rather than the external manifestation of neurosis.'

If we focus on the pain and suffering, then we are drawing attention to this state and easily become immersed in it. We are giving the suffering extra power and importance. But this is not the whole person. When we communicate with the Self beyond the suffering, with that which is fiee and at peace, then the person in pain can begin to experience their own essence, to find themselves as they really are. Then the pain belongs to no one, it just is. This is also true when we relate to someone who is angry or upset. If we respond to their anger then it can incite the situation even more. For the anger is not the whole of us, it is only a manifestation of one aspect. When we relate to the whole being then it has a chance to respond.

Finding Our Own Path

Finding a meaning to life can sometimes involve hitting the bottom before we start going up again. How much worse are we willing to let things become before we make our search a serious one? There are very few people who have made Self-realization their goal, most of us are content with whatever piece of happiness we can carve out for ourselves. We normally settle for so little, suffering in silence rather than journeying onwards to a more fulfilling and awake place. For what makes us so special that we, personally, could actually discover a whole new way of being? Are we not just like all other people who make do with their lot?

As we become aware of the limitations of the mind we can no longer be content with the ways of the world – the misconceptions and endless dramas – instead there arises a searching for a deeper meaning and purpose. The superficial and insensitive qualities of life begin to fall away and we start to seek a new way of being.

Making this change means stepping out of the norm, out of the ordinary mainstream of life and moving in an individual direction, one that we create for ourselves – we move to the beat of a different drummer. For this is uncharted territory, different for each one of us. There are no familiar codes of behaviour, no signposts or instructions, no set rules on how things should be done. And although the ways of the past have become less meaningful, the new ones have yet to become clear.

At first we may try incorporating the old with the new, but it is not so easy to discuss opening the heart while sitting in a noisy bar with a pint of beer! People with whom we normally associate, or things that we used to do, no longer seem to hold our interest as they used to, we are beginning to seek a different fulfilment. It is not as if we are rejecting the past, but rather that we are expanding beyond our previous experiences. Impetus and motivation are now arising from a selfless place instead of a selfish one. Thinking with the heart is like learning how to use new sense interpreters, new means of perception, even new parts of our mind. The old way of reacting to a situation no longer fits, but what is the new response supposed to be?

Each one of us has to find our own way of dealing with the flood of feelings, insights and sensitivities that result from opening the heart. It is a time to listen to what our inner self is saying, to trust that within the uncertainty a new way is opening that we can follow. For most it includes a releasing of old wounds, a forgiveness of past hurt, a letting go of limitations and dogmas. There is a willingness to be caring, receptive, loving and tender. It may also mean a change in lifestyle to a simpler or more humble expression. Some may choose to work for the peace movement, to do volunteer work with the homeless, or some other expression of compassion and care.

Debbie remembers when, many years ago, she was participating in a peace march in London. 'Walking in front of me in the march were a group of thirty or so elderly people, some with walking sticks, most with white hair. As they walked along in the rain and cold winds, this group was singing the most glorious songs, their voices filling the air. They were members of a Welsh choir and had travelled to London for the day's march. What struck me most deeply was how, considering their age, none of these people would be likely to see world peace in their lifetimes, yet their enthusiasm and commitment was as great as that of any younger person. They were outwardly expressing the deepest desire in their hearts.'

The Fourth Chakra

We have already discussed how, when functioning through the third chakra, we manifest self-importance and the need for power. The ego is dominant. Yet also inherent within the third chakra is the potential for transforming that power to one that is nourishing and benefits all beings. This is the consciousness of the fourth chakra, simply known as the heart chakra, the awakening of universal love. The above story is an example of such love.

This chakra marks a complete shift in consciousness away from the defensiveness and protection of the self to the transformation of those energies into empathy and compassion for all beings. It is the integration of the understanding that, although we may have different appearances, in our hearts we are one; there is an inner connectedness, a loving kindness and respect that arises naturally. As Tarthang Tulku says in *Gesture of Balance*, 'It is in the heart center that our inner nature grows to fullness. Once the heart centre opens, all blockages dissolve and a spirit or intuition spreads throughout our entire body so that our whole being comes alive.'

The consciousness expressed here is the emergence of the true individual, one who sees no division between anyone or anything but is focused on the essence in all. This is a tender and gentle place from which we can give of ourselves more fully to the world for there is no fear of attack, of being manipulated or dominated; there is no fear of losing ourselves – it is not possible to lose what we have found for it is our true nature. This develops a very different way of relating to the world, it is a shift of awareness from self to awareness of other than self. It is no longer enough to think about ourselves first before others, to see life only as it revolves around our personal universe. The awakening is of a deep sensitivity towards all beings.

Love has always been associated with the heart, from red Valentine cards to graffiti scratched on the walls. But this portrayal is of the romantic heart which can just as easily be broken as it can be radiant. The heart we are talking about at the level of the fourth chakra is not this fragile romantic symbol, but that of the all-encompassing, unconditional love that is alive, indestructible, permanent, embracing. It arises as we release the hold of the ego, for here the ego begins to become redundant – operating from such a self-centred place is no longer appropriate but actually hinders true communication. We want to step aside and respond in a different way, rather than following old reactive patterns of behaviour. It is not as if the ego disappears entirely, but its influence in our lives becomes less noticeable.

In its wake there can be a feeling of vulnerability, as if we were wide open with nowhere to hide. We may cry more easily, whether because of a simple tear-jerking movie or because of the level of suffering we see around us in the world. A softness develops, a tender-hearted quality that sees through the bravado and persona to the gentle, somewhat insecure being inside. This vision begins to awaken love for all beings, whoever they may be. For we are no longer seeing others only from our own perspective, relating to their effect or not upon our lives, but we are seeing beyond the differences to the place where we are the same, where we are all equally vulnerable and tender.

The Healing Heart

The lack of such love is the cause of so much pain, disease, unhappiness and distress. Discovering unconditional love is the beginning of a healing process, a healing of that which has been buried deep within. To be healed means to become whole, to come into a state of unified wholeness. This implies an embracing of all the different parts of ourselves, whatever they may be; it means accepting our guilt, shame or anger, that this is who we are, just as we are, and it is OK. For unconditional love has to first start at home.

How often have we turned away from ourselves because we cannot bear to know who we are? Can we look in the mirror without judging what we see? It is extraordinary how many of us do not like ourselves. We wish we had different hair, were a different shape or size or height, had a different nose, legs or waistline. Yet bar plastic surgery or a miracle from above, this is who we are! Self-dislike, unworthiness and low self-esteem are so common. What a waste it is to spend so many years wishing we were different instead of accepting who we are and getting on with developing our potential.

Obviously it can be overwhelming to try and love ourselves all at once, but if we can start by just acknowledging what is there and beginning to accept that this is it, then we may find we are not so bad after all. Acceptance comes before love. It is a process of taking it step by step, accepting each bit at a time, rather than trying to do it all at once. There is no point in putting ourselves down and generating further pain and guilt by trying to love ourselves but not succeeding. Applying pressure to make us love is not how it is meant to be! Let us just start with acknowledgement and acceptance and the rest will follow.

Many of us say, 'Oh, I love myself.' We go around hugging people and saying how much we love them, and yet we are not really loving anyone. What we are loving is what we are getting from each other, we love others because they love us – when we are not loving ourselves then we need to receive love from somewhere else. If we are to experience unconditional love then we must let go of the conditions. In accepting ourselves unconditionally – just as we are, embracing all the many aspects of our being, both painful and joyful – then we can also accept others in the same way.

Love brings up everything that isn't love, in order that it may be healed. For when love is present, then it provides a safe place for all the pain, fear, confusion and grief to come into the light, to be embraced and transformed. So when our issues arise, such as anger or neurosis, then if we can accept that this is who we are rather than denying it, we have the chance to heal. Normally we have such a well-protected image of ourselves! Loving ourselves means being able to go through that image to the reality of who we are in our entirety, complete with all our neuroses and paranoia. It is not a narcissistic ego-based love that only loves the good bits. It is an egoless love as it also embraces that which is dark and ignored.

Loving ourselves is about forgiving ourselves for all the hurtful and painful things that we have experienced. We feel unloved, but is it because we are not loving towards ourselves? We find fault with others, but perhaps it is because we are not happy with our own lives. Normally we hold on to our pain and blame someone else for it, but what we really need to do is to forgive our own actions. For no matter how bad the hurt or abuse has been, no matter how much we may disagree with others, if we start with forgiving ourselves then we will find we can also forgive others more easily and accept them for who they are. Let us remember what it has taken to get where we are, what we have been through, and bless ourselves for who we are!

This takes courage, confidence and acceptance, until we are able to fearlessly embrace our own darkness. But as Benjamin Franklin said, 'He that falls in love with himself will have no rivals!' If we can come out of our minds and into our hearts then it is like coming out of a tunnel into a bright and clear world, where we can see in all directions. We expand into a world of compassion and understanding for we are no longer obsessed with being right or being accepted.

We can actually develop a whole new relationship that we never had before, one in which we can become our own friend. Being lonely implies we have no relationship with ourselves, rather we are wanting life to be different, we are not at ease with what is. Loneliness is a painful state but it can be transformed. A woman was once complaining to her teacher that although she was a part of a community she felt very lonely and had no friends. Her teacher replied, 'Then be a friend.' The world is a community – in becoming a friend we will have friends, in giving we receive.

Being alone implies we are at one with the joy and love of life, for alone is really *all one*, our oneness with ourselves is a oneness with all. Joy is a word we do not hear very often for most of us have been too well indoctrinated by the idea of confession for what we have done wrong, rather than celebrating what we have done right. When we open our hearts there is a natural joy that arises and fills our whole being. We want to sing, to listen, to rejoice, to smile. All this goes against the grain of our being introspective and repressed. But discovering our hearts is a very joyous occasion!

It is the re-connecting with our purpose, for the love in the heart is that supreme guidance that leads us from hopelessness to hope, sadness to joy, anger to laughter. The healing that occurs is of a re-mission, a re-discovery of our mission or purpose in life. As the heart opens the healing takes place on the deepest level for we are no longer involved with pain or difficulties from our own viewpoint, but we can see the inter-dependence of all things, how each thing is intimately connected to the next. We are moving from a selfish and self-orientated place to one of awareness and sensitivity to the whole.

The Lotus in the Mud

An image we can use to understand this further is that of the mud, the stem and the lotus. Such a beautiful flower as the lotus does not grow in pure spring water or clear mountain pools, but instead it emerges out of dirty water, thick with mud. Similarly, the lotus is there within each of us, ready to grow out of our mud, for it is the flower of our enlightenment. The stem is our commitment to freedom, our willingness to grow and to truly transform, it is the energy that motivates us. The stem and the flower emerge because of the nourishment they are receiving from the mud. This mud is the unconscious, made up of all our repressed, hidden and denied issues. We work towards the flower as we work with our mud, as we accept and embrace ourselves. We water our flower with our willingness to work with ourselves, to acknowledge what we find. The stem is the commitment that even when things are difficult and there are hard times we can still love.

In the West there is a tendency to over-indulge in our issues, to get immersed in our neuroses and ego-centred nature, but this process does not necessarily help us grow. The mud can become our friend, it can become fertile – we do have the capacity to turn dirt into gold – but we have to first let go of our neurotic and habitual mind, the mind that wants to cling to the mud. Then the creative, awakened mind that is hidden can rise up and we can become a true human being.

Maturity is the ability to enter into our mud, into our issues, and to embrace them. It's saying yes, this is who I am and it's OK, it's absolutely OK. Embracing ourselves means that all the mud – the issues that we're carrying around with us – can actually become fertile ground, can become the very source of nourishment that feeds our flower. If the stem is our commitment, then it will arise as we know that we really want to be better, that we really want to be free; it is a commitment to our own happiness.

If we think about how a tiny little weed can grow through six inches of solid concrete to reach the light, then we know transformation is possible. We may think that our issues are so big we cannot get through them, that we are too fragile and precious. Yet we have all been through so much, we have survived so much, we are not so delicate! We can emerge, no matter how hard it may be. The acceptance of ourselves is our anchor, the weight that grounds us in reality.

So if we can love ourselves, unconditionally, then we are entering into the core and the essence of who we are. We can be fearless, trusting, and have a clear mind where there is no chaos, confusion or doubt because we can look directly at whatever arises. It is almost impossible to work through the mind to a higher understanding without awakening the heart, as the heart releases the mind from the trappings of the ego. The heart is the essence. Negativity and confusion are of the mind, compassion and understanding are of the heart. So the heart enables wisdom to come to its fruitition. Out of the mind and into the heart.

Love and Fear

As we open the heart so we find our fears beginning to dissolve. For love and fear cannot co-exist within us, they are opposing states that cancel each other out. Fear is contractive and exclusive, a pulling in towards ourselves and a pushing away of others; while love is expansive and encompassing, a reaching out and embracing of both self and others.

Until now fear has been the dominating factor in our lives. Fear of survival, fear of pain, fear of being different, fear of loneliness, fear of death, even fear of fear. We fear to give love in case we get hurt, we fear to give money in case we are left without any, we fear to give thoughts in case v;e are seen to be wrong. We even fear being happy! How many times have we heard ourselves say, 'I'm feeling happy now but I know it won't last', or 'There must be something wrong, I feel too happy!'

In the process of seeing fear for what it is we have to deal with all that has been holding us in this contractive state – the habitual patterns and behaviour, the neurotic tendencies, the anger, pride and ego. Some habitual patterns protect us from being hurt, buffering us from our real feelings. By providing a familiar reference point we do not have to deal with the implications of freedom. Thus our habitual patterns enable us to keep our heads down and avoid the brightness or harshness of life. Like an ostrich we think that by hiding our heads in the sand no one else will see our neuroses!

Fear can be understood as meaning False Evidence Appearing Real. In other words, we become consumed by what we think is going to happen, by what we think lies in the future and we spend our time feeling anxious and worried about this. But it is a false reality as it is not happening now, therefore it is not real. Does all the worry and fear actually change or solve anything? For we are being fearful about something that has not yet happened, and may not even happen! And if it does, then is it not enough to worry about it then, let alone now as well?

In order to work with the fearful and neurotic tendencies of the mind we need to develop fearlessness. This is the ability to look directly into a situation without being threatened or undermined by it. If we react with fear we are thrown into a panic, whereas fearlessness means diving into the fear itself. In most incidents we will find that the fear has no real ground. If we give it power it overcomes us, just as when we are walking in the dark and we think we see a snake but it is actually a coiled rope. It may be necessary to take a deep breath, to gather our courage together so we do not react so quickly to the fear.

This gives us the opportunity to check within ourselves and see what other options we may have, for fear is never the only one. Imagine a wild animal stuck in the middle of the road, caught under the car headlights and paralyzed with fear. What other alternatives does that creature have? Fear shows us our limitations and can thus enable us to go through it and to develop a deeper level of flexibility. The physical expression of fearlessness is one of both arms expanded open wide, the heart therefore open and all the organs unprotected, defenceless; it is an openness that invites unity and togetherness. Fearfulness is a position where the arms are crossed, holding together, keeping the heart closed, it is a position of excluding self against another.

Debbie remembers when she and a friend were once walking in the hills and came across a herd of wild black cattle. 'As we proceeded we became aware of a huge bull in the middle, and that it was preparing to charge at us! There was absolutely nowhere to hide – not a rock, tree or wall – nothing. I found somewhere as I crouched on the ground behind my friend! He then reached into the depths of his fearlessness and stood his ground, arms relaxed and open by his sides. The bull charged, then veered away a few feet in front of us. Fearlessness – an open heart – is recognized by all creatures.'

Living with an open heart means living with and in love, in a state of expansiveness and fearlessness. The word love has been defined in many different ways, from mother love to sexual love, from desire to domination. Here we are not using it in the romantic or ego-centred sense, for that is always bound and limited. Rather we are seeing it for what it really is – a universal truth. If love is real then it must surely be unconditional. If it is not unconditional then how can it be love? Is it need? Or expectation? How can we say, 'I love you but . . .'? If we believe we love someone and then they take their love away, do we still love them? Or is our love conditional upon them loving us? If it is, then can we honestly call it love? Are we simply in love with what another is giving us, or with the idea of being in love? We can certainly have strongly romantic and caring feelings, but if we are living in the head then such feelings will easily be influenced by the events surrounding them, thus we love one minute but not the next.

When we experience an open heart then our love becomes natural, constant and free of limitations. There are no objects for the love, it is not based on any one thing. If the one we love takes their love away then we are still able to love them, for our love is not dependent upon its being returned. It may not seem so easy to love when we are not receiving, but it is a love that reaches towards all beings, all things, simply because they are alive, have life within them, are expressing who they are in this moment of their lives. It is like a flower that is always giving of its scent, whether anyone is smelling it or not. Others do not have to be or do something special in order for us to love them. And they do not even have to know.

However, living in such a way can arouse suspicion and doubt as most people are not used to being treated fairly, to being considered or really listened to. Thus they may question our motives. When we first start experiencing this inner softness it is natural to want to share it, to try to show others where they are going wrong, how they could respond differently and thus find greater happiness. This invariably incites them even more! For if beneath all our actions is the one desire to be happy, then who wants to be informed that their very attempt at finding happiness will in fact lead them to further suffering?

How often have we seen this in the loving mother who only

wants the best for her child, but in the process is smothering and confining until the child finally rebels and pushes away? Tact and care are needed so that we can express ourselves without causing resentment or rejection. There is no need to overpower others – we do not need to control or rule, but simply to be open and honest.

Compassion

From unconditional love comes compassion, the deeply felt response within us that wishes only that all beings become free of suffering, as well as the causes of that suffering. However, longing for another's freedom can be a way of ignoring ourselves – we also need to find our own freedom from suffering. As Thich Nhat Hanh says in *A Guide to Walking Meditation*,

> You can experience compassion for others only when you are compassionate with yourself. You feel this compassion when you see that you are bound to the frame of worry and sorrow. You understand that worry and sorrow cannot help you to solve any of your problems. Instead, they obstruct your peace and joy.

Loving kindness is the active aspect of compassion, where we are able to act in such a way that there is a connectedness to freedom as a result. This is the skilful means we mentioned earlier, the action that brings understanding, comfort, nourishment and insight. As Thich Nhat Hanh continues, 'Decide to let worry and sorrow fall away. If you want to, you can – like taking off a raincoat and shaking of all the raindrops that are clinging to it.'

But let us not fool ourselves, for it is certainly easier to have compassion for our child or our close friends than it is for ourselves, or for someone who abuses or hurts us! As Khentin Tai Situpa points out in *Way To Go*,

> At present our compassion is quite restricted, being easy to engender when we are happy and almost non-existent when we are faced with problems. *Unrestricted* compassion is immutable and it is directed towards absolutely all beings within the cycle of existence, whether they be friend, stranger or enemy.'

To know how to respond in any given situation it helps to be able to turn the tables, as it were, and to see things from the other person's perspective. How often does the ego normally allow us to do this? To step into someone else's shoes and feel what they are feeling, whether it be pain or joy? For if we do this we can no longer accept our way as being the only one that is right. We are immediately aware that the other way is also right, which then makes neither one right or wrong! The empathy for another's feelings takes us out of our own limitations, enabling us to expand, to open, to listen and receive. When this happens, compassion is the natural response. For how can we feel hatred towards another when we can feel their pain?

As Tarthang Tulku so eloquently says,

> In the beginning our compassion is like a candle – gradually we need to develop compassion as radiant as the sun. When compassion is as close as our breath, as alive as our blood, then we will understand how to live and work in the world effectively and to be of help to both ourselves and others.

It is important to remember that we are not talking about a passive or docile attitude when we talk about being compassionate and loving. Compassion can be very dynamic. Springing from a place of tenderness does not stop it being vibrant, powerful, active or effective. For instance, if we see someone being beaten up it does not mean that we just stand back because we have such loving kindness for the abuser and accept what he or she is doing. But there is a sense of detachment so that we can be helpful rather than adding further negativity to the situation. Instead of getting angry and demanding punishment for such a person, we can see that they get help or support to enable them to work out their difficulties without hurting anyone else.

Detachment is not the same as being indifferent or uncaring. Rather it is the deepest expression of compassion as we are free of personal involvement and can therefore give more appropriately and fully. Indifference is a smokescreen we put up to hide our real feelings behind and it is the negation of love. What we are looking at here is that love can have many expressions, not just the soft and passive ones we normally associate with it. As events and issues arise we can respond spontaneously and genuinely in whatever way is most skilful for all concerned.

There is a tender sadness that can overwhelm us as we confront the pain in this world. No longer seeing right and wrong, war can lose its relevance, for who are we fighting if not ourselves? Political issues can seem petty in the face of homelessness and starvation; execution or life punishment appears to be just a way of avoiding our own darkness by dismissing it or locking it away. The governing machinery of this world does little to accommodate the fact that we are human, all inter-connected to each other, that we all feel pain and want love and attention. It is extraordinary how seriously we take this relative reality to be, exploiting others to make ourselves seem bigger and better, killing or hurting so as to gain power. But power over what? Is all this not the clearest expression of ego? Of the need to experience love?

From compassion we come to commitment, for as much as we may be well-intentioned and honest in our attitudes, our commitment to living in the heart must be constant – it takes great courage and motivation for there is much that can hold us back. It is easy to be distracted, especially when we are dealing with the day-to-day reality of family dramas, work, paying the rent, the car breaking down, meeting deadlines. All of these provide mental conflict and stress. To remain steady and true to the heart means having an unwavering and firm commitment to ourselves and our freedom. While all things are transitory, this remains real and constant, beyond all limitations. When one person finds peace then that is one less person suffering.

The Warrior

The image of the warrior is becoming an important symbol in the Western world, for it is an image that evokes all of the mythological past yet also goes beyond the stereo-type macho hero. There have been images of the warrior in many of the major traditions, such as the samurai in Japan, the brave in Native American lore, or King Arthur in England.

The warrior of the heart is one who is not afraid to feel sadness and to cry, nor afraid to show tenderness or vulnerability. Yet at the same time the warrior can walk fearlessly in the world with dignity, sanity and basic goodness. The warrior bears insult and injury and responds with compassion. When there is a closed heart then bravery is all show and bravado; with an open heart it genuinely arises from tenderness. Here the bravery is due to the courage to simply be oneself, to live without deception, but with acceptance and connectedness. For real strength is not to be found in the manifestations of life – in power, money or even weapons. It is to be found in the deep silence and peace within, and in the ordinariness of every day.

As Thich Nhat Hanh says in *Every Breath You Take*,

> We are very good at preparing to live, but not very good at living. We know how to sacrifice ten years for a diploma, and we are willing to work very hard to get a job, a car, a house, and so on. But we have difficulty remembering that we are alive in the present moment, the only moment there is for us to be alive. Every breath we take, every step we make, can be filled with peace, joy and serenity. We need only to be awake, alive in the present moment.

The warrior's strength comes from the love that pours through every cell of the body, from the commitment to truth and honesty. It is this commitment that keeps the warrior focused, enabling constant confrontation with all of life's ordeals; it is the motivation to serve all beings equally that keeps the warrior committed. This is done, not because the warrior has become enlightened and is therefore free of all fear, but because there is a full acknowledgement of the fear. If we have fear then we also have the potential to be fearless. Acknowledging our weakness is what gives us strength. We can become flexible and responsive.

In *Shambhala, The Sacred Path of the Warrior*, Chogyam Trungpa points out how the key to warriorship is not being afraid of who we are; nor do we need to be afraid of the threat the world situation presents, to protect ourselves against

others. Rather we can go beyond ourselves to seeing the
whole. He says,

> A great deal of chaos in the world occurs because people don't
> appreciate themselves. Having never developed sympathy or
> gentleness towards themselves, they cannot experience harmony
> or peace within themselves, and therefore what they project on to
> others is also inharmonious and confused.

Debbie recognized this while she was working with the
elderly. 'I had reached a point of burn-out, being asked to
do anything, even something very simple, was causing me
distress. I had nothing left to give. At first this was very
upsetting as I wanted to be able to give without any limitation. But when I realized that in accepting that there were
limitations, then I was able to turn what appeared to be a
weakness into an inner strength. It is acceptance, not denial,
that strengthens us. In so doing, I found a deeper source of
giving than I had touched on before.' As Chogyam Trungpa
says, 'What the warrior renounces is anything in his experience
that is a barrier between himself and others. In other words,
renunciation is making yourself more available, more gentle
and open to others.'

Living in the heart means being able to fearlessly take risks,
to live more on the edge of life rather than needing to be safe
and secure. We can be fearless warriors! We can play more,
for we are in the world but not dependent on it. Life becomes a
friend rather than something to be constantly fighting or con-
tending with. The science-fiction writer, Ray Bradbury, said
recently how he lives in his heart because,

> If we listened to our intellect, we'd never have a love affair. We'd
> never have a friendship. We'd never go into enterprise because
> we'd be too cynical. Well, that's nonsense. You've got to jump off
> cliffs all the time and build your wings on the way down.

Decisions that are made with the heart are quite different to
decisions made with the head. Heart decisions have no ego
involved, no closedness or prejudice, but they may have little
logic! They can also be deceiving. Debbie remembers a situation when Eddie wanted to do something and she responded
by saying, 'No, I really don't feel this is the right thing, my
heart is saying no.' Eddie went ahead anyway and it was the

best thing that could have happened! It made Debbie realize how much of her ego had been involved with what she had said. Heart decisions may seem irrational, illogical and go against the mainstream, and yet they feel right. And if we follow them it will be right. Head decisions are obvious, rational ones, but they do not always turn out as we planned. Learning to follow heart decisions is a part of the warrior's path.

In particular, the warrior is very ordinary, there is no sense of needing to be special in any way. We have forgotten that being ordinary is OK. We have forgotten that we do not have to be special in order to be lovable; that everyone in this world experiences pain and suffering, not just us; that we can be compassionate and loving even if we are hurting. Being ordinary is a selfless state, one in which we do not have to be something, to draw attention to ourselves. Being ordinary means having time and space for others, without comparing them to ourselves. To compare simply causes unnecessary conflict and how can this help us? There is such incredible beauty in being ordinary. This is what being mature means. Enlightenment is ordinary – it is our natural state. Neurosis and fear are extraordinary. Dare we become ordinary and drop the extra?

Living with Love

If love is a letting go of fear – and as all of the great teachers have always been described as being complete manifestations of love – then it implies that the state of enlightenment as seen in these teachers is a totally fearless one. This state of complete fearlessness manifests in the heart, arising spontaneously as a result of letting go of all that which is in doubt, is anxious or uncertain. If we are receptive and open, then to be with someone who is so completely loving and fearless like this invariably touches us in such a way that our own fears can also drop away.

Is this what happened when Jesus healed the blind? Was he not an embodiment of love? Did the pure love that was so pervasive within him completely embrace the sick and enable them to drop their own problems and pain, to see their own light? As Huston Smith says so eloquently in *The Religions of Man*, of the effect Christ had on the early Christians,

> If we too really felt loved, not abstractly or in principle, but vividly and personally, by one who has united in himself all power and perfection, then the experience could melt our fear, guilt and self-concern forever.

For love of this quality embraces all equally, giving for the joy of giving and serving for the love of service. It is a love that has no boundaries, shining like the sun, for that is its very nature.

Bringing love into our own lives on this level is obviously quite rare, and few of us have ever been with such a totally loving person. But perhaps we can most align ourselves to such love by loving ourselves, by tuning into the love that is already within us. For if we do not feel love within, then can we honestly say we love anyone? If we can really accept ourselves then we can also accept others – once we have seen the madness within our own minds, nothing that may spring from any other mind can surprise us! It is the love for who we are that brings us closer to the love, the essence, in all beings. As Emanuel Swedenborg said, 'Our distance from Heaven is in proportion to the measure of our self-love.'

Therefore, even if we have not physically been with a truly loving teacher and felt the radiance coming from such a being, we can nonetheless feel the love in our own hearts and thus experience the essence of such divine power. For the love is the same, wherever it may be manifesting from. Just as the planet is in orbit, the sun rises each day and the waves wash the shore, so we breathe the air and feel the earth beneath our feet. Ultimately we are each a part of the love that sustains all things. If we can make the journey to our own heart then we will find ourselves in the heart of all.

The Metta Bhavana

There is a simple meditation practice that is particularly designed to help us develop a greater experience of open heart and loving kindness. It is called the Metta Bhavana or Development of Loving Kindness. In this meditation we discover that to truly practise unconditional love we have to start by loving ourselves, just as we are, fully and unconditionally. This is not always very easy, but it is essential! We have to look at all that which is stopping us from loving ourselves, and be able to accept and be at peace with that.

Start by finding a comfortable sitting position, whether cross-legged on the floor or sitting in a chair (with the feet flat on the floor), with the spine upright and the eyes closed. Hands are resting in the lap. Take a deep breath and relax.

1. In the first stage of the practice you begin by loving yourself. Do this by taking your attention to the heart area and then silently repeat to yourself, 'May I be well, may I be happy, may all things go well for me.' Acknowledge any opposing thoughts that might come to mind: reasons why you should not be happy, or not be well, feelings of guilt or shame and of not being worthy of such love, or your inability to receive. Acknowledge these and let them go. Continue doing this and repeating. 'May I be well, may I be happy, may all things go well for me', for the next few minutes.

2. In the second stage direct your loving kindness and compassion towards a near and dear friend. Choose someone within 20 years of your own age and of the same sex, simply to avoid parental or romantic feelings, and to allow true unconditional love to develop. Now direct your loving kindness and compassion towards this person and silently repeat, 'May they be well, may they be happy, may all things go well for them.' Acknowledge any feelings of competition or jealousy that may arise and let them go. Continue this for a few minutes.

3. In the third stage direct your loving kindness and compassion towards a neutral person, someone for whom you have neither positive nor negative feelings. You may not even know his or her name, for when we know someone we immediately have a specific feeling about them. So it may be

just someone who works in a store, or delivers the post. Find this person and hold them in your heart and let the unconditional love flow towards them. 'May they be well, may they be happy, may all things go well for them.'

Here we feel the love for the unknown. In reality we are all one, so even with this neutral person we are one. Feel the love expanding towards even those who are unknown to you. This may seem odd or difficult at first, but keep going for a few minutes.

4. In the fourth stage direct your loving kindness and compassion towards one with whom you are experiencing conflict, where there is negative communication between the two of you. This may be a relative, friend or colleague. Hold this person in your heart and expand your loving kindness and compassion even to them. Let your acceptance and love flow towards them. 'May they be well, may they be happy, may all things go well for them.'

Holding this person in our hearts, we expand our forgiveness, acceptance, our love and our compassion. Feel your heart opening, no matter how hard it may be, towards this person, for the next few minutes. For we are one with them also. Let us remember that pain is born out of ignorance, and we can forgive ignorance. In forgiving others, we are ultimately forgiving ourselves.

5. In the fifth stage, start by holding these four people in your heart: yourself, your dear friend, the neutral person and the one you are in conflict with, and feel such unconditional love and compassion towards all four equally that if you were asked to choose one in preference over the others you would not be able to do so. Your love is truly unconditional.

From these four you now begin to expand your loving kindness towards all other beings. Realizing that there is no difference between yourself and all others, you radiate further and further. Ultimately we are all one. Your love extends outwards, slowly reaching all beings, so that you are unconditionally loving all, whether they be a murderer or a saint. The love in your heart expands to all beings, everywhere. 'May all beings be well, may all beings be happy, may all things go well.' May all beings be at peace and may I be at peace with all beings.

5

Riding the Elephant, Lassoing the Tiger

As we open the heart and begin to view our world from a place of tender-heartedness, then we can truly work with the mind. It is difficult to see the intricacies of the mind clearly and know how to deal with them while we are so engrossed – this is like trying to see the whole wood when we are already surrounded by trees. But from the heart, the depth of our being, we can have a clearer perspective.

We are able to observe the many different personalities the mind plays out – how it produces each one according to circumstances – and to see the underlying motivation for our actions: what it is we want to get for ourselves out of the things we do, what unconscious desires are being manifested, what hidden motivations there may be. The human mind is full of neurosis, doubt, confusion, and all these get bottled up in such a way that we feel quite mad at times. In fact everyone is a bit mad – we just manage to keep it well hidden from each other! We think we must be the only ones, but if we could only know that we all think the same then we could even laugh at ourselves. We are just very good actors!

All the different personalities we express are like animals in a jungle, each with their own particular characteristics, habits and territories. We may be like the elephant, slow and persistent, not giving way to anything in our path so that we achieve our desires in a steady but somewhat stubborn way. At other times we may be like a tiger, restless and quick to attack, reacting to irritation and annoyance by growling or rearing up against our enemy. Yet we can also be like a snake, slithering our way unnoticed through the undergrowth until we reach our goal and then attacking with venom. Our own jungle of wild animals is alive and well within us and we tend to invoke any one of these creatures as an unconscious response to, or a way of dealing with, the circumstances we are facing.

Riding the Elephant, Lassoing the Tiger

Learning how to ride the elephant or lasso the tiger is the process of being able to deal with these symbolic animals in the mind, instead of their having such control over us. Rather than being the victim of our neurotic and discursive mind states, we can learn how to watch the habitual patterns arise without being subject to them. We cannot force the mind to change – that would be like trying to catch the wind – but we can become objective and actually witness what is taking place. As we discussed earlier, it is difficult to really be a witness from within the mind itself, but if we are in the heart then it is like having a ringside view from which we can watch the dramas unfold! And if we can approach our difficulties with a loving heart then we may find they are not as big or as menacing as we had thought.

To be able to heal or change the tendencies of the discursive mind that pull us in so many different directions we need to see what is arising without judgement or prejudice. Having witnessed what is taking place we can then begin to accept and even embrace these discursive aspects of our being. As the understanding of the mind develops, we grow into greater completeness, removing that which causes fear and confusion. As the heart awakens we begin to weed out the negative tendencies in the mind and to cultivate a flowering garden!

Before we look at how to deal with the many variances of the mind, how to actually ride and lasso such wild and tempestuous personalities, let us take a closer look at those creatures that reside in this mind jungle of ours, and what they represent. Having looked at their more limited and darker qualities – those that are holding us back – we will then explore making friends with them and integrating their strengths and attributes.

The Elephant

The elephant is normally associated with being a slow but loving animal, not bringing harm on anyone, simply minding its own business as it goes on its way. Plodding through life without much excitement it has its routine and likes to stick to it, staying within familiar parameters and avoiding change wherever possible. However, this slow and repetitive action can often become lazy and indifferent, even uncaring, for the elephant stays on its path regardless of whether there is anything in its way or not, sometimes creating great disturbances as a result. For instance, situations have occurred where a village has been built on an old elephant path and the elephants have just kept on walking, despite any huts or buildings standing in their way!

The elephant is also known to rampage when incited, trampling over anyone or anything, stampeding towards its goal and wreaking havoc in its wake. It then returns to its slow and steady ways, as if there had never been such an outburst. And we are left in awe at the wild and disregarding nature just displayed. Is this really our loving and quiet old elephant? For surely the elephant has a keen intelligence that would disparage such behaviour?

Looking a little deeper, we might be able to discern the level of insecurity that such conflicting attitudes are expressing. What is the need to be so detached that we become indifferent, even dismissive to others around us? Is it not a hiding of our real feelings, for to express them might prove overwhelming? Can we cope with the reality of our feelings or is it easier to deny them? And to what extent are we maintaining control, not just over ourselves, but over others as well, by being so removed and separate from personal involvement?

The elephant personality is the one who never says much, but when it does then everyone stops to listen, for great words of wisdom can emerge from this most venerable and ancient of creatures. Penetrating insight is one of the elephant's greatest attributes. Unfortunately, the lazy behaviour of this animal can also be reflected in a lazy mind! How often do we expect to hear something meaningful and find ourselves listening to banality instead? As the elephant speaks so rarely, we patiently await its words.

The elephant may not even be aware of the effect it is having by remaining so quiet. But what insecurity encourages us to be so over-powering? Do we feel so superior that to join in normal conversation is beneath us? Or do we need to make ourselves appear so very wise by being quiet because actually we can think of nothing to say? Invariably the elephant personality, until it matures, is unsure of its feelings or how to express them. It is therefore fearful of change as this usually means having to confront or voice an inner opinion. Change is a threat to the safe facade we have created around us that protects us from exposure. Change means movement and this demands energy.

Yet when change comes and the elephant is aroused enough what happens? There is a great eruption, a stampede through our world. Why? Is it because the feelings within that have been gathering for so long simply run riot when released? Is the idea of change so fearful? The control is gone and in its place is a deep fear of being caught without the normal means of defence. By wreaking havoc around us we can distract others from seeing clearly; they think they are at last getting some real emotion but fail to see that this is still a form of protection, a facade.

This is a repressed personality, a holding back of ourselves in order to appear better and more capable. For are not the real feelings ones of insecurity, fear, self-doubt and a lack of confidence? The very opposite to what we would expect to find in an elephant? By appearing so strong and majestic, are we not hiding the fact that within us there is actually a small and frightened mouse?

The positive aspect of the elephant energy is that it can be used to help us move ahead without being distracted. In the Eastern tradition, the elephant is the remover of obstacles and is symbolized by Ganesh the elephant god. For no matter how slow or how rampaging it may be, there is no doubt that the elephant can remove anything that stands in its way. Therefore the elephant energy can be used for us to overcome that which is holding us back, to clear the path of our fears and habits so we may proceed, to shift those hindrances that are blocking us. The very slowness and steadiness of the elephant is to be honoured as this can be transformed into a considerate energy that does not rush blindly through life, but applies mindfulness. Within this action is the mature wisdom born from years of experience. The elephant has the ability to tap into a deep knowledge that reaches bach through the ages.

The Tiger

Here we find an animal that is restless, pacing back and forth, is quick to attack and become angry or aggressive. Yet the tiger is also known to be crafty and sly, using camouflage to be able to creep ever closer to its prey. This creature certainly does not protect or hide its feelings like the elephant does! Any incitement, however innocent it may be, and the tiger will instantly make itself known, pouncing on the unsuspecting victim, growling and snarling at being disturbed. Yet beneath this outer persona we find a purring cat, happily licking its paws in the sunshine, full of contentment with itself!

Is this us? Are we so quick to attack that we may not even be aware of why we are attacking? Is our anger so readily at hand that it is the first response we have to any situation that does not please us? Are we so irritated by even small and petty things that we just want to lash out? And if so, then what is the cause of such anger? What has made us so defensive, so unable to express love, gentleness and sensitivity, except to those who have won our loyalty?

Instant anger of this nature invariably points to a deep frustration and sense of injustice with life. Somehow things never live up to our expectations, we never seem to get what we want, everything always seems to be slightly against us, irritating the desire we have for a serene garden in which we are the ruler. We eventually become so locked into our way of viewing life that we fail to see it is not the only way. And what we miss altogether is that maybe no one is actually attacking us first.

In other words, are we demanding more from life than we think we are getting? Such demands give rise to tension and stress, to an attempt to achieve what we want at any cost. We are unable to surrender, to let go and allow life to unfold by itself, in its own way and at its own pace. We believe that we have to carve out our own reality as we do not have the trust that it will happen without our interference. This is the fighter, the one who uses sly means as readily as aggressive ones. This is the part of us constantly attacking whatever appears to stand in our way, for fear that if we do not attack first then it will overpower and stop us from achieving our goals.

Yet beneath the aggression, is there not a gentle soul longing to be recognized? Is our fighting not a round-about way of trying to attract attention and love? Have we been so badly hurt, abused or mistreated that the only way we know how to get what we want is by being aggressive or even vicious – to scratch instead of kiss? Is not our real nature a nurturing and playful one that loves the sunshine? What fear makes us cover up such loving qualities? Are we able to let our defences drop enough that this softness and warmth can emerge?

The tiger is known for its power, but this power need not be aggressive. It can be transformed to give us courage and strength on our journey of self-discovery. It is an assertive quality which, instead of being directed in a violent way by pouncing on innocent passersby, can be used to assert our commitment to awakening, to energize and stimulate our practice. When the tiger energy is transformed then its power brings purpose and can be used for the benefit of all. The inner softness then emerges as compassion.

The Monkey

Our playful friend the monkey likes nothing better than to leap from branch to branch, from tree to tree, exploring here and there but never staying anywhere too long. What a game life is! How boring to walk on the ground and how much better to fly through the air and discover life's plentiful fruits! Without a doubt there is great intelligence here, one that can grasp new ideas or solve problems without any difficulty, but then how dull it is to get stuck in one place and not be able to run around!

The monkey in our minds does just that, leaping from one thought to another, especially when we are most wanting to be quiet and sit still. A monkey cannot stand school work, or being in an office, or even meditating! It has to be off and out, leaping from thought to thought, drama to drama, doing something and then something else, creating endless distraction. This is the mind that is fickle, restless, constantly creating new playgrounds without having fully explored the one it is in, always believing that the best place to be is somewhere else other than where it is. For the monkey mind loves entertainment and spends its time looking for ways to be excited, for new adventures, games or activities to be engrossed in. Is this why we are so obsessed with television, with partying, or with psychics and therapists? For to be quiet with our own inner silence is an unknown experience for the monkey mind. To delve a little deeper is rare.

First, let us not sound too serious here! It is wonderful to have the playful nature of the monkey, for many of us are far too fearful to be so carefree and spontaneous. But when the monkey is dominating us to the point where our minds are always on the go, always searching for new pastimes or are lost in mental chatter, then what is it that we are not wanting to deal with in the present, or what is it that we are running away from in the past? What drives us to be so distracted? Are we wary of becoming too serious, of allowing ourselves to penetrate the meaning of life, rather than just skimming its surface? What are we afraid of finding if we do stop to look? Is it not ourselves we are running away from?

Maybe we think that by constantly distracting ourselves we can avoid the pain or conflict that is there, just beneath the surface. Or perhaps there is a guilt or shame, a story of abuse that is too great to reconcile. And somehow we believe that if we just keep moving from one thing to another, keeping the issues superficial and playful, we will not have to deal with who we really are, will not have to confront our fears.

The monkey is not only playful but also very intelligent and resourceful. The monkey energy can therefore be used to keep us going during difficult times, enabling us to see a situation for what it is without getting too caught up in the drama. The intelligence of the monkey clearly perceives that laughter and play are the best remedies to life's more serious scenarios! Getting entrapped in dogma or difficulties leads us nowhere, whereas laughter enables us to lift ourselves up and breathe fresh air.

The Snake

This is the creature that fills our nightmares, the archetypal symbol of all of our worst fears. The snake has the image of being full of hatred, not discriminating in its object of attack. But most importantly it can creep up on us whenever we are not looking, using the energy of the underworld to reach its target. It therefore feels dark and sinister and we are vulnerable, merely a victim in its presence.

The snake represents that dark and sinister side of us, full of resistance for anything that threatens our stability or protection. We see it reflected in racial prejudice – the whites against the blacks, Hitler against the Jews, conservatives against the hippies. When we are fixed in the belief that we are the only ones who are right then anything that threatens such a belief will be seen as the enemy. Beneath the surface we plot our ways to crush and defeat so as to be rid of such a threat. This hatred is due to a deep fear of what the threat might represent, a fear that it will undermine and get the better of us in some way. Before it can do that it has to be stopped. The true snake has no fear of the enemy. Like a hired gunman, it is single-minded in its purpose, unstoppable until its goal has been reached.

The snake represents that darkness within, the unconscious fears and paranoia that lead us to project it outwards, to think that if we can just annihilate such darkness then we will be free. Yet the darkness is actually within us, not out there in other things, people or races – these are simply symbolic. So where has this hate come from? What deep fear is it hiding? And why do others appear as such a threat to us? What insecurity or doubt in ourselves are we avoiding by blaming others?

This attitude of hate implies a closed heart, an obsession with war and revenge, the belief that one man can hurt another without hurting himself. Ultimately it is the egotistic belief that we are all separate from each other and that therefore I am better and more important than you. Is it possible for us to look a little more honestly and to see the connectedness between all beings, that there really is no separation between us and therefore no cause for hatred? Can we confront the darkness in ourselves and take responsibility for it as being our own, so that we do not need to blame others? Can we find the inner security that does not need to be all-powerful in order to be safe? Can we transform the hate to discover the compassion and love that is actually our true nature?

For the snake is also the symbol of transmutation, of Phoenix arising from the ashes – when we transform the dark and hateful qualities we enter into light and love. The snake can therefore be our closest ally, that which clearly demonstrates our fears and yet gives us the power to go beyond them. Transformation of this energy is the greatest as it represents the dark within us being transformed into the light. Such transformation comes through an acknowledgement of our fears and darkness, for normally we prefer to deny these feelings even exist, putting on a brave front instead. If we can talk about our fears we might find we are not so alone, that each of us has similar issues. In sharing we can discover that fear is mutable and that being vulnerable is safe. From acknowledgement can come acceptance, and in acceptance there lies the potential to transform – darkness cannot stay dark when light is shone upon it.

The Bird

There are many more animals in our jungle that we could discuss, but the garden bird is one of our favourites. What delicate little creatures, so fragile and yet so colourful, twittering here and there, pecking and picking, jumping with alarm, fleeing from danger, always on the alert! Yet what a beautiful sound they have, a song that fills the air, a gentleness and joy that touches all.

How easy to recognize the bird! Immediately the image comes to mind of a little lady, dressed in bright array, maybe with a hat decked with colourful flowers or fruit. She is thin and agile, eating only a small amount at any one time, seeming even to pick at her food rather than to eat it. She twitters, rapidly talking about one thing or another, yet without really making too much sense. She moves constantly – from the table to a chair, from the chair to a vase of flowers, from the vase to a picture on the wall, adjusting, straightening, fixing. When startled this figure will quickly dart away, maybe to the kitchen to make a cup of tea and calm her nerves, or to potter in the garden where she has infinite space to keep moving. She is not happy when confronted with stormy or loud emotions, preferring to retreat to the safety of her room above. This wonderful image is of a figure we love and want to protect from harm for she seems so fragile.

How about the bird in ourselves? Do we fly away from difficulties or confrontations? Are we in a fearful state, always on the lookout for possible danger? Do our neuroses get the better of us so that we can never be still, are always moving, but without clear direction? Do we pick at life, as if fearful of actually taking a bite big enough to sustain us? And when things get rough, do we slip out of the door and quickly retreat upstairs to our safe haven? It is as if we are in life but not quite a part of it, maintaining our own means of protection and ability to flee at any time so that when life becomes a threat we can quickly be gone. Our wings take us off the ground, away from dealing with reality, and into the fantasy realm in the clouds. How much more pleasant to dream the hours away than to have to come down to earth and actually participate in it!

There is certainly a sense of great freedom here, but does the bird not fly *away* from something, rather than flying *to* something? What has made us so ungrounded and nervous that we are never really present but always slightly distracted? Can we find a stillness and a strength within that does not need to fly, yet is just as free?

The bird sings the song of truth, removing fear as its music fills the air, encouraging us to look upward to the heavens for inspiration. The transformation of the bird energy is the ability to consciously fly freely, without being attached to any one thing. The soaring eagles and hawks that grace our skies represent the power and strength of such freedom, the selfless objectivity that can see in all directions, can see all viewpoints equally, observing the world without being subject to it.

Making Friends with Our Jungle Occupants

To ride the elephant or lasso the tiger implies we have made friends with these wild creatures and they are no longer able to dominate or frighten us; they can even enlighten us! In other words, as we work with our minds and come to identify and accept all the different roles and personalities we play, so we need no longer be under their influence. But this is definitely easier said than done. It is not, for instance, just a matter of sitting down in a nice armchair in front of a log fire and slowly running through our reactions and responses of the day to see what categories they neatly fit into! To rise above the discursive and reactive mind we have to apply insight, motivation, commitment, determination, wisdom, impartiality and compassion, and we will probably have to practise all of these a great deal, every day, until they become a natural part of our lives.

Thankfully, as we proceed in making friends with the many aspects of our minds, there are some guideposts to help us along. In fact the transformation of one's mind from a sleeping and reactive state to an awakened and creative one is the core of most of the world's spiritual and religious teachings so we have a variety of directions to choose from. As we explore these teachings, although each path has its own unique approach and attributes, we may find none more suited to our task than those arising from the East, such as Buddhism and Yoga.

For instance, the Buddha put more emphasis on the taming of the mind – on the overcoming of our habitual patterns – than he did on any other subject, so there are clear and plentiful directions on how to deal with this. He taught how it is the mind that brings such endless suffering with all of its discursive desires, yet it is also this same mind that can lead us to a state of divine bliss. With the view we now have from the heart, we can hardly disagree with such a statement! We have already seen the suffering we put ourselves through, and we know that in order to deal with this confusion we have to develop a greater sense of awareness and compassion. And we also know, intuitively, that this will bring us to a state of awakening, of freedom.

We may also find solace and direction in the teachings of Yoga, for here, as with the guidance of the Buddha, we find a map outlining and detailing a way for us to go that has been well trodden by seekers over the years. It even has a 'You Are Here' arrow, to ensure that we do not get lost! In this way we can learn how to walk fearlessly through our jungle!

The Buddha's Eight-Fold Path

After the Buddha realized awakened mind, his first teachings were to help us understand the predicament we are in as we flounder this way and that in our confused minds. He began by teaching the Four Noble Truths. The First Truth explains how life is in constant change, nothing is permanent, and how this fact can cause great suffering. Such suffering reaches in all directions and affects all beings for it is natural to cling to permanency and resist change. For what we call suffering is in reality no different to the facts of life – transition, movement, birth, death. It is our reaction to these that causes the pain.

The Second Truth explains how this condition of resistance is primarily because we are in a constant state of clinging and desire as we want, we get, and we still want more! The play of desire, satisfaction and loss is endless. This resistance to change is also because of the belief that we are all separate and independent from each other, a belief which can lead to wars, hatred and revenge.

The Third Noble Truth is that such resistance can be relieved through a release of desire, a letting go of who we think we are. However, if we were able to simply cut off our desires there would be no problem, but as we all know this is not so very easy – desires have a way of slipping back into our minds while we are not looking! So in the Fourth Noble Truth, the Buddha outlined a way of living which can guide and support us through our journey of surrendering the ego.

This teaching is the Eight-Fold Path. Following it asks for our full participation, for it is not something that someone else can do for us whereby we are simply passive receivers. This path is one that demands action and personal motivation, through which we can come to understand ourselves and become free of our illusions. The clue to the entire teaching is practice, for without application this path remains a purely intellectual exercise, one that we can mentally grasp but do not personally experience. Through practice we are able to tame the wild animals in our minds, to make friends with them and bring them into our hearts. The teachings are just guidelines, suggestions to help us; they provide us with a raft to reach the other shore but are not the shore itself. Each of us has to discern what teaching is appropriate for ourselves and what is not.

The implication of this path is that every aspect of our lives can lead us to greater awareness. As Pema Chodron says in

The Wisdom of No Escape, everything we do can help us realize our unity and oneness with all things, all life.

> We can wake up to the fact that we are not separate; the energy that causes us to live and be whole and awake and alive is the energy that creates everything, and we are a part of that. We can use our lives to connect with the energy, or we can use them to become resentful, alienated, resistant, angry or bitter.

1. Right Understanding

The first step along this path is Right Understanding or View. By this we mean the insight into and acceptance of the reality of existence, in particular the inter-dependence and inter-relatedness of all things. If we are under the impression that each thing or each individual is separate and independent of all others, then we have full justification for all the greed, hatred and desire that dominates our lives. But in understanding the connectedness – how one thing cannot originate without relationship to another – we see how all things are in constant dependency with each other at all times. For instance, in the human body, each single cell has awareness of and is related to every other cell – in this way they can operate as a functioning whole. And there is no difference between the relationship of our cell structures and the relationship between all things in the world.

In developing this understanding, our view changes. We can no longer live in a selfish and isolated way, building our defences against a fabricated enemy, holding grudges or resentments, having more for ourselves and thus causing others to go without. Our view expands to include all beings as a part of, and no different to, ourselves.

We also become acutely aware of how desire dominates our minds, while simplicity, contentment and humility are rarely a part of our vocabulary! As Thomas Merton says in *The New Man*,

> Humility is absolutely necessary if man is to avoid acting like a baby all his life. To grow up means, in fact, to become humble, to throw away the illusion that I am the center of everything and that other people only exist to provide me with comfort and pleasure.

But freedom from desire does not mean we have to become wandering monks living in caves! What it means is recognizing the cause of our discontent and not giving it attention so that we can connect with a deeper level of contentment. This is the recognition of the inherent beauty that is within each thing, a beauty that transcends both perfection or imperfection. Right understanding implies grasping the underlying factors that are keeping us bound to the endless cycle of pain and happiness, suffering and joy, and being free of their influence.

2. Right Aspiration

The second step is Right Aspiration or Intention. Here we are asked to look within our hearts to find the commitment to, and motivation for, what it is that we really want. Do we have the wholehearted belief that we can become free, can awaken to our true nature and can end our suffering?

The understanding that this is possible is essential, for without it we will not take the path to finding freedom, we will prefer to stay in a conditioned and limited state. In knowing that freedom is our goal we also have to honestly believe that we can be free. The egotistic mind may try to stop us, may make us think we are not capable of such awakening, but within our hearts we need to be connected to the knowledge that enlightenment is our natural state or we will have no impetus to continue. Right aspiration is right intent, the arising of a genuine and heartfelt motivation to become free of the limitations that so dominate us.

In practice we can see this as the development of generosity, compassion and harmlessness, otherwise known as the absence of thoughts that are greedy, hateful or harmful. As we have already seen, desire is the cause of endless suffering due to its constant demands. Greed is closely associated with desire but highlights even more strongly the sense of separate existence. For greed is desire for oneself over and above others; it is a taking, not a giving. The extraordinary thing is that when we do start giving – and here we mean giving in whatever way is possible for us, whether materially or with a smile – it gives us far greater joy than taking does.

Hatred is a deeply destructive and damaging state, actually poisoning our own system far more than it may the person it is directed at, for we are the ones carrying the emotion. Hatred highlights our separation from others as it creates a dark and venomous condition; it colours our minds so we cannot see clearly. Transformation takes place when we can see the inter-relatedness between all beings, for how can we hate something that is a part of us unless we are really hating ourselves? If we see good in the world then let us rejoice; if we see hatred or darkness then let us look within ourselves. Compassion arises naturally as hatred dissolves and we experience our unity with all beings.

However, even if we have overcome hatred we can still harbour harmful and cruel thoughts. Developing harmlessness means having the deepfelt longing to bring no harm to anyone or anything, but to live our lives in a considerate and sensitive manner, seeing how we can be constructive and creative rather than destructive. This means practising harmlessness with ourselves as much as it does with others. *Ahimsa* is the Sanskrit name for harmlessness, a quality that is rare and precious. It is not always possible to live without creating any harm. For instance, in a relationship or marriage separation pain is almost inevitable, but we can act with love, integrity and honesty and try to find the way of least possible suffering. As we learn not to resist change and movement, so the pain of separation can be lightened.

3. Right Speech

From developing the more altruistic attitudes of under-standing and aspiration, we now come to look at our personal behaviour more closely. Our speech is an immediate and clear indicator of who we are (not just the person we would like to be!), especially when we say things without really thinking, thus expressing the unconscious energies. How often have we heard it said that the truth comes out when a person is drunk? Is it because the protective defences and inhibitions are gone, and in their place we find the 'real' person?

If we can begin to watch our speech we will soon see what

we are really saying. For instance, can we manage to hold a conversation without talking about ourselves? Without bringing attention to ourselves? Without saying I? Some friends tried this with a famous actor. They met this man for dinner and purposefully talked about everything except him in order to see how long it would take for him to turn the conversation around to start talking about himself. It took all of two minutes!

We can also observe how violent or critical our language is. Do we need to swear a lot? Is it pleasant for others to hear this? Or are we, perhaps, trying to make ourselves look better by putting up a big brave front, appearing macho, or even by putting others down? And most importantly, how often are we deceiving people with our speech – exaggerating, lying, or distorting the truth? And maybe even deceiving ourselves in the process?

It is not as if we have to become absolutely honest, never uttering a word unless it is the whole truth. But we can develop an awareness of what we are saying, of the underlying intent, and of any hidden emotions that may be expressed in our tone or volume that we are not consciously aware of. How much aggression or anger is really in our voices? Do we have to talk so loudly, and if so, then why? Who are we trying to impress? Is the gossip and idle chatter really constructive or is it actually destructive? And can we discover the beauty of silence? How often do we use our voices to hide ourselves from being alone with who we are? If we do have any of these qualities, let us not condemn ourselves, but rather see how we can change and bring about a greater level of mindfulness.

4. Right Action

The fourth step is Right Action or Discipline. Following right speech, this continues our need to look closely at our behaviour, to develop an awareness of how self-serving or essentially destructive our actions may be. Beyond the obvious of looking after our basic needs such as food and shelter, how many of our actions are actually covetous, selfish and self-centred?

Remember we are not being told that this is what we *have* to do, but rather that these are ways we can work with ourselves. Here it is firstly suggested that we refrain from any action that may hurt, harm or kill another, therefore practising harmlessness or *ahimsa* as discussed above. Practising harmlessness in this way also means being gentle and taking it easy with ourselves.

Secondly, it is suggested that we refrain from taking that which is not given, to avoid stealing. This is not always as simple as it sounds, for few of us think of ourselves as outright robbers! But there are many other ways of taking that which is not given, especially emotionally or psychologically and it demands greater self-honesty to see this. Can we be more considerate? Third, we are advised not to commit sexual misconduct. What is meant here is any form of sexual act that is without consent or causes grief or harm to another person, such as rape, adultery or abuse.

These three right actions all have the same idea at their root and that is the development of a basic respect towards ourselves and others, a respect that honours the feelings of all beings and does not wish to harm them in any way. This implies accepting others just as they are, simply, without judgement or discrimination. As Chogyam Trungpa says in *The Myth of Freedom*,

> If there is a tree, there must be branches; however if there is no tree, there are no such things as branches. Likewise, if there is no ego, a whole range of projections becomes unnecessary. Right discipline is that kind of giving-up process; it brings us into complete simplicity.

5. Right Livelihood

This takes into account not so much our actual occupation as our attitude towards it. Obviously, if we are aspiring to lead a life where we are practising harmlessness, then to be a butcher or to sell alcohol would be difficult occupations to follow! However, we see harmfulness taking place as much in a business deal as we may do in a butcher's shop. What is more important here is asking ourselves to what extent we use our occupation as a way of identification, making it the reason for our existence, making it the goal rather than the means. And what level of ego-gratification do we seek through our occupation?

The world is set up so that unless we are in a prison or a monastery, we pretty much all have to pay our way! That means needing some form of work. This is why our attitude is so important. Are we working in order that we can just gain materially, or are we doing it so that we can have the time in which to meditate or help others? Is our occupation more important than our quest for enlightenment? Do we become the work itself – I'm a doctor, I'm a writer, I'm a teacher, thus feeding the ego – or are we able simply to be who we are regardless of our occupation?

Right livelihood is important as it represents our whole attitude to life. If our external activity dominates our world then we become nothing if that work is taken away, we are left useless and deflated. On the other hand, if the work is done without personal attachment, then who we are within ourselves remains free of labels and identification.

One of the most important aspects of spending time at an ashram or spiritual community is that whatever our job is outside of the community makes no difference, we are not identified by our content for within the community all are equal. Thus a top executive might be asked to clean the toilets, while a shop assistant might be asked to landscape the gardens. In this way we quickly discover that it is not what we do that is so important as is our attitude. Cleaning the toilets is no different to being a president, unless we are personally identifying with and wanting something from the activity.

6. Right Effort

Here we move from dealing with our behaviour to looking at our personal development. To proceed we have to have the will, determination and energy to do so. This means applying effort to recognize and work with our more negative reactions, such as anger and fear, and the effort to transform them into love and fearlessness. For these things do not happen on their own! If we are only putting effort into personal achievement and accumulation then this is a form of deluded effort. The effort we need to apply is so we may become *less*, not more, it is so we may become free of the illusions that are keeping us bound. It demands that we apply honesty and vigilance, for the ego will do all it can to maintain our illusions!

Right effort is the will to keep going even when times are tough, for such times are sure to happen. The path can sound so clear and straightforward when we read about it, but our own personal experiences along the way invariably include conflicts and difficulties, steps backward, moments of hopelessness, even a wanting to give up altogether. Is this not one of the reasons why so few people ever travel this way? It is a demanding path to follow, asking that we look into our darkest corners and have the courage to confront whatever is there. To experience an awakened state we need to recognize all that which is holding us back, to acknowledge this and release it. The effort to continue is essential. It is also most rewarding. As Henry David Thoreau said, 'I know of no more encouraging fact than the unquestionable ability of man to elevate his life by a conscious endeavor.'

Effort is also commitment, the focusing of our determination and activities in one direction. Without this there can be hesitancy, doubt, the chance to draw back, as well as an apathy and general disorientation. With commitment there is energy and clarity, the will to proceed and overcome hindrances; there is faith and trust. As Goethe said, 'Whatever you can do, or dream you can, begin it. Boldness has genius, power and magic in it.'

7. Right Mindfulness

This, in effect, calls for us to become aware of ourselves and the causes of our actions, aware of our thoughts and the causes of such thoughts. It is the development of the witness, the observer watching what is taking place and being able to see what is behind the scenes or to read between the lines. It is also a way of relating to all things in a precise and complete way. Further, it is asking us to observe ourselves in such a way that we are able to connect with who we really are beneath this outer persona. Marilyn Ferguson says in *The Aquarian Conspiracy*, 'Anything that draws us into a mindful, watchful state has the power to transform . . . Mind, in fact, is its own transformative vehicle, inherently prepared to shift into new dimensions if only we let it.'

Mindfulness is something we can practise at all times, in every moment of our lives. It simply means to become focused and aware, a bringing of the mind into the activity. Try washing the dishes with such awareness – noticing the play of the water, the movement of the brush or sponge, the light catching the clean china – and see if it does not become a marvellous act of creation, a dance of the elements, rather than a duty or dirge! All of our actions can become mindful, from dressing to eating, from urinating to talking, all can be imbued with a sense of the sacred.

As mindfulness develops it brings a genuine simplicity to our world, it is the addition of consciousness to our every action. It gives us a space in which to be aware and clear of what we are doing, and whether such action is in the best interests of all concerned. However, we may need help in practising this, and for that meditation is recommended, whether it be for a few minutes every day, a few hours, or even a longer period of retreat. In the silence and solitude of meditation we begin to see ourselves, to connect with who we are, without interruption, and thus to develop a basic mindfulness.

8. Right Concentration

This brings us to the final step, that of Right Concentration, also known as absorption. Without effort, motivation, understanding and mindfulness being developed, our meditation is meaningless and will simply serve to enhance the ego further. But when these qualities have been integrated into the fabric of our being, then meditation becomes a deeply meaningful activity. Right concentration is the focusing of energy so completely that we, as individuals, no longer have a separate identity. We become absorbed in a non-dualistic way of being. Slowly, step by step, we remove the obscuration, like cleaning the dust off a mirror, so that we may now glimpse our true reflection. As we become more deeply focused in meditation, entering into the stillness of the mind which is true concentration, awakening can take place. We discover our true nature, the reflection of that which has always been there.

In this way, the Buddha outlined the means through which we can tame our minds and come to know ourselves as we really are. Similar to the Eight-Fold Path, and also arising from India, are the teachings of Yoga.

The Four Main Paths of Yoga

Many of us associate yoga with exercises – a form of movement that stretches, tones and balances the whole physical system – but that is actually only one aspect of this ancient teaching. There are also other forms of yoga because we, by nature, are different to each other. No one path will be right for us all. The teachings describe four main types of person: that of the reflective and intellectual, that of the emotional and devotional, that of the active and physical, and that of the scientific and experiential. These basic differences need to be accommodated, so various approaches to the path and different techniques are taught. Each one of us can find that which suits us most. Gopi Krishna, in *What is Enlightenment?* describes the purpose of following these teachings by pointing out, 'The goal of yoga is this union with the universe of consciousness . . . it is a herculean achievement, more full of adventure, risk, and thrill than the longest voyage in outer space.'

Jnana Yoga

This is, primarily, the path to awakening through the intellect (please note – this does not mean the same as being locked in our heads!). Rather it is using the intellect to transcend the intellect. It is the way of knowledge and philosophy, of reason and understanding. Naturally this path can easily become an intellectual fantasy without real application, so the important emphasis here is that of *living* the understanding, putting into practice that which the philosophy focuses on. In other words, if the understanding is deep enough it will affect our entire being and way of life. Thus our intellectual penetration can become a means to freedom from all intellectualization! For the aim of this path is to be able to separate that which is real from that which is unreal, to discern between ignorance and knowledge, to see the difference between our normal and worldly self and the true higher Self that lies within. It is to expand our mundane mind into the greater mind. To do this, three steps are advised.

The first step is that of listening. This is usually translated to mean listening to the teachings or philosophies, to join in study groups and reflect on the ancient teachings. But it also means being able to really listen and hear both ourselves as well as another person. When we can listen in this way, when we can hear what is being said and that which is not being said, then we can penetrate into the nature of the mind itself. If we are not really listening then all we will hear is what we want to, or what fits our own views, we are not being open to receiving or learning.

The second step is that of thinking or reflecting inwardly. Here, what is heard is applied so that true discrimination can develop. Appropriate reflection enables us to see our behaviour and attitudes and to penetrate their meaning. Why do we, for instance, think in terms of 'my' body, or 'my' family, or 'my' job? For where is the 'I' to be found? Where is the true 'I' beyond the outward manifestations? If we persist enough along this path of self-reflection we will soon discover that which is eternally within us, that which is beyond the 'I'. However, no matter how profound this discovery may be, there is still a sense of duality.

The third step is therefore the integration of this knowledge so that there is a merging with the Self to the point where there is no longer any distinction or separation. All sense of duality dissolves. If we do not come to this point in Jnana yoga then we remain locked in mere intellectualization. Integration into the heart is essential for the teachings to have any real meaning. It can be achieved through meditation on or contemplation of that which is real. With a completely quiet mind the essence of truth is revealed.

Bhakti Yoga

This path is for the emotional devotee, one for whom love is all-encompassing and consuming. It recognizes that it is love that nourishes and transforms the human mind into the supreme open heart. Bhakti yoga therefore takes this vital experience and directs it entirely towards God, towards that which is pure awakened consciousness. Through devotion, prayer, ritual and the complete absorption with the love of God, we surrender the ego and become one with the divine, thus transcending all dualities. For instance, through chanting the sacred sounds and repeating mantras our consciousness is uplifted, the mind quietens and merges with the sound. The inspiration that each individual may feel towards the symbol of their religion or belief can be used to encourage and pro-voke transformation. This creates a deep peace which in turn brings a flow of healing and ecstatic energy. When we love in this way, then the love purifies our vision and we become universal in nature.

Most of us only see love in its personal form such as the love for our family and friends. To conceive of a love that is greater than this mortal plane is often beyond our comprehension. Hence, the path of bhakti can easily be seen as weak and over-emotional, only for those who have no real intelligence. In fact, in its true application, bhakti yoga demands a tremen-dous letting go of our own issues and neuroses in order to be able to surrender. Remembering that love and fear cannot exist together at the same time, then how can we even begin to surrender to love if we are in a state of fear? In the place of fear comes trust, faith, and finally divine unconditional love. In other words, the path of bhakti involves a merging of the mind into the heart and is therefore a true opening of the heart. It is certainly not a simple exercise of the mind, or an excuse for intellectual ignorance!

The path to being consumed by such love takes many forms. For some it will be in the silence of prayer where the love in the universal heart is found. For others it is in the repetition of rituals that overflow with the symbols of God's many manifestations. These symbols each represent different aspects of the divine nature, as no one single symbol can represent such a magnanimous concept. Through such images we can connect with a particular aspect of divinity and embody it within ourselves, thus transforming our neuroses into attributes.

For instance, for the Christian it may involve repeating the name Jesus or Mother Mary, or visualizing Jesus during prayers. Devotional practice for the Buddhist may involve the repetition of the mantra 'Om Mani Padme Hum' which can invoke compassion, or the visualization of various deities. For the Hindu, it may involve repeating the mantra 'Hare Krishna, Hare Krishna, Krishna Krishna, Hare Hare'. This connects one to the love of Lord Krishna. In each case it is a merging with the form that awakens the power of love.

The path of the bhakti is filled with stories and myths relating the miraculous and glorious nature of the divine; with the recitation of God's name (in mantra or prayer); with meditations focused on becoming one with such beauty; and with the experiencing of the many different aspects of divine love. The true bhakti realizes oneness with God and the divine, but chooses to act as the devoted lover.

Karma Yoga

This is the path of work, action and practical application. By this is meant not only the work we may do between nine and five, but is applied to all of our activities, at all times. It is interesting to note that, for most people, being idle is difficult if not wholly boring, for we are not only physically attuned to work, but we also find it very hard to be still with ourselves. For instance, retirement often brings with it many complex difficulties as we try to adjust after so many years of feeling valued and important at work. But karma yoga suggests that our money-earning work is only one part of our lives and we can actually practise a different kind of work at all times, regardless of our employment status.

Karma yoga is working in such a way that we are surrendering our ego within the action, giving up our selfish purposes and becoming one with the divine by focusing only on what we are doing in this very moment, here and now. If our activities are only for our own benefit then this is not karma yoga, for our motives will be selfish and therefore tainted with expectation. And if we are doing the work for the sake of others but are suffering at the same time, then we are becoming martyrs, and this is not the point either. It is when we are working for the sake of work, doing it for the love of doing it, giving without need of return, and in such a way that others will benefit, that it is karma yoga. Our activity becomes a form of devotion and selfishness becomes redundant. We enter into the body, thus enabling the mind to be free of neurosis and discursiveness.

In traditional yoga ashrams (spiritual communities) and in other monastic settings we usually find many hours a day devoted to karma yoga, whether it be gardening, cleaning, cooking, and so on. Very often we are asked to do the same chore over and over again, despite its having been correct the first time. In one ashram we know, an elaborate and beautiful flower garden is constructed each year, only to be swept away by the monsoons and replanted again the following year! This might seem ridiculous and one cannot help asking why they do not construct a wall or some other means to stop the monsoon having such an effect. Or why not move the garden to a safer spot? But the teaching lies in the work, not in the permanency of the plants. In the *Bhagavad Gita* it says that karma yoga is a surrendering of the fruit of all action to the divine. Similarly a tree grows tall and strong and then gives of its fruit to all who want it, without wanting any for itself. In fact, humans are the only ones who, so to say, eat of their own fruit.

In Tibetan Buddhism there is a wonderful story of Milarepa, a young adept whose teacher, Marpa, asked him to build a house. Having completed the job, Marpa then told him to tear it down and start again. This happened seven times! It was only after the seventh house had been built that Milarepa finally went beyond his constantly questioning and neurotic mind and entered into a state of egolessness, wherein the activity was done for its own sake, not for some preconceived ulterior motive (such as having a house). Karma yoga and Bhakti yoga can here be seen as quite similar as they both aim at the complete dissolution of the separate self and the ego into the divine Self. Bhakti yogis achieve this through devotion, karma yogis through selfless activity.

A true karma yogi (practitioner) aims simply to be in the present moment, doing each job fully and with complete awareness. This applies to whatever activity is being done. Some years ago, Debbie was participating in a seven-day zen meditation retreat. A few hours a day were given over to work, but there seemed an inordinate amount to do. As her teacher walked past during one such work session, Debbie protested at being asked to do too much. Her teacher responded, 'There is never too much to do. We do what we are doing and when that is finished we do the next thing. There is only too much if we are living in the future. By living in the present we simply do what is there to be done.' Laziness is thus an issue that does not arise!

We can discover the meaning of karma yoga at times when we may be feeling depressed or irritated, but instead of venting those feelings we start to clean windows, sweep a floor, or dig the garden. It does not take long to find that the feelings have become less important as our mind becomes absorbed in the activity. When we are really mindful of the activity then the mind does not drift into distracting thought patterns.

Raja Yoga

This is often known as the king of yoga (*raja* actually means king) as it is perhaps the most comprehensive of the four yoga paths. Raja yoga is for the experiential students and for those needing to see an effect, as it can be proven scientifically, thus expelling any doubts and misgivings we may have about following such a teaching. We are asked to explore, experiment and discover for ourselves how we can reach deeper understanding and eventually complete liberation. We are never asked to believe something without proof of its validity.

The father of raja yoga was said to be an Indian pundit

known as Patanjali. He outlined eight basic steps, which combined together are aimed at training each aspect of one's being from the physical to the mental, emotional and spiritual. It is interesting to see how closely linked these eight steps are to the Buddha's Eight-Fold Path outlined earlier. In hindsight, perhaps, we can see that the many paths to liberation are not so different after all!

1. The first step of raja yoga is known as *yama* or self-restraint. By now we may have recognized how our addictions, habitual patterns and neurotic thinking are not exactly helping us to tame our jungle! So here we are taught how to deal with our behaviour by resolving to no longer kill or harm others in either thought, word or deed; to not lie to or deceive others; to not steal or take the not-given; to not give in to addictions or sexual activity that may harm others; and to not allow ourselves to be greedy or avaricious. By taming our actions we are correspondingly able to tame our minds and all the various disturbances that arise.

2. The second step is called *niyama* and here we deal with our own personal lifestyle. It is suggested that we become physically aware of our condition by practising personal cleanliness and order (without becoming neurotic!); by being content with whatever happens; by developing self-control so that our passionate and neurotic tendencies do not have a hold over us; by studying the teachings and understandings of those who have gone before us; and by contemplating and surrendering to the divine, whether through prayer, meditation or devotion. These two, *yama* and *niyama*, cover the ethical and moral training that lays the foundation for our progress. Let us also remember that we are human and that we can only do our best! Although we can apply effort to explore ourselves, we should not become guilt-ridden or judgemental if we miss the mark. Rather than punishing ourselves, let us be able to learn from our mistakes and move on.

3. The third step is that of *asanas*, or physical exercises known as hatha yoga. Asana literally means seat posture, so the emphasis here is to practise certain postures in order to develop our seat, or our ability to sit, and thus to meditate. If

our physical body is under duress and tension we will not be able to sit still and meditate and therefore develop insight so easily. Instead we will be constantly disturbed – moving, fidgeting or aching. Through the various asanas we become flexible and are able to strengthen and relax, loosening the whole body, so that it is free to move or to sit without stress. Asanas also help calm the nerves, oxygenate the blood and the brain. Thus our physical being will be more at ease, not only in meditation but also in any other activity. This whole system of working with the body is now used throughout the world to promote relaxation and good health.

4. The fourth step is *pranayama*, or the practice of regulating the breath. The act of breathing not only sustains life but also reflects the rhythms of the universe, as seen in the seasons changing or the movement of the waves on the shore, the tides, and the cycle of the moon. These rhythms form the movement of the universe as a living whole and humankind is an intricate part of this whole. In developing various breathing practices we are working with our *prana*, the life force or universal energy that flows within and throughout us. Working with the breath also calms the nerves, balances the energetic forces and creates a physical state of ease, eventually creating a state of deep tranquillity. In the ancient Indian texts it says that if we can control the flow of the breath then the mind can also be regulated and controlled, leading to greater equanimity and peace.

5. The fifth step is that of *pratyhara*, meaning the withdrawal of the mind from the senses. This is usually accomplished through practising deep inner conscious relaxation, a state that is not sleep yet is more profoundly relaxing than sleep. When we project our mind and senses outward we know only too well what a world of distraction and confusion we can enter in to. Here we do not identify with the objects of the world, nor with our thoughts or desires; we are not subject to our needs but develop the clarity of objective awareness. By going within there is an inner tranquillity; we dissolve into a world that is truly peaceful. Eddie's book, *Inner Conscious Relaxation*, gives more practical advice on how to practise this level of withdrawal. It is essential to develop deep relaxation in order to be able to meditate or focus our minds with

concentration. Without being relaxed the inner stress will stop us from going further.

6. The sixth step is that of *dharana*, the fixing or concentrating of the mind on one thing or object. Through the previous steps we have learnt to deal with our behaviour, our bodily stresses and strains, and to withdraw from sensory distractions. Now we have to deal with the mind and its constant chatter, daydreams and memories. Left to itself, the mind would never be quiet for it feeds on endless discursiveness – it is the monkey mind, the aggressive tiger or the slow-witted elephant! Any of us who have practised meditation will know this, for as soon as we want to be quiet the mind starts up yet again!

To enable the mind to become still we are advised to learn how to focus so completely on one thing that there is nothing that can disturb us. The object of attention – perhaps a candle flame, the rhythm of the breath, a repetitive sound such as a mantra – is not as important as the idea that the object is just a tool we can use to focus. For instance, we can sit and gaze at a candle flame positioned at eye level, then close the eyes and try to visualize the flame within. If not a flame then we can do the same concentration practice with a flower. By becoming completely absorbed in the object the mind is able to be at rest. Pratyhara teaches us to withdraw the mind from the senses, while dharana teaches us to be one-pointed in this withdrawal so our energies are not scattered and we can penetrate more deeply into our true nature.

7. The seventh step is that of *dhyana*, or meditation. While we are focusing on an object there is still the awareness of the object, there is still duality, I and it. In dhyana the sense of separation dissolves, there is a complete merging so that there is no self-consciousness left. Duality ceases to exist, the various fluctuations of the mind begin to settle. Thoughts are like the waves on the ocean, with meditation creating a calm sea where the waves become smooth. We cannot see the depths of the ocean if the waters are choppy – it is only when we become calm and quiet that we can penetrate into the depths of the mind.

As we become more skilful, so this freedom from the neurotic mind becomes natural, we are no longer under the control of our fears but are at ease with ourselves. As the ego lessens, so our understanding deepens. This leads to samadhi, to true contentment and freedom.

To practise meditation we can sit either in a cross-legged posture on the floor or in a straight-backed chair with both feet on the ground. Our hands are in our laps, our eyes closed or half-closed. There are then any number of techniques. For instance, we can follow the flow of the breath and count at the end of each out breath from one to ten and back to one again (one number per breath); or we can witness the thoughts as they come and go without getting involved with them; alternatively we can repeat a mantra or prayer over and over, becoming completely absorbed in the repetition. The technique is less important than the absorption of the mind in the practice. When the mind becomes still the technique drops away and we experience true meditation.

8. The eighth step is that of *samadhi*, the highest of experiences. It occurs when the meditation is effortless, profound and uninterrupted by thoughts. Here the mind is completely absorbed in ecstasy and is one with God, with the Self that is within each of us. The light of truth radiates and fills every cell of our being. There is no thinking, there is no object, there is no self. There simply is. It is not as if we have no mind *per se*, for what is the mind but a bundle of thought patterns and desires built up inside us? Rather, we grow out of the adolescent, grasping mind, and mature into one of wisdom, compassion and equanimity. All the meditation and yoga we do is in order for us to reach this state.

From the Jungle to the Ocean

We have come a long way from recognizing the creatures in our jungle and the madness of the human mind! The jungle is there and it is real, just as the different feelings, fears, worries, and guilt appear real that we harbour within ourselves. But perhaps they are only real on the relative level? For as we follow the guidelines that can lead us out of the jungle we discover that there are actually fields, mountains and an ocean, all awaiting our exploration. There are more places to go than just inside our heads. We can explore the wondrous heart, expand our understanding, enter into the body, enjoy its dance and enable it to become free of its stresses; we can even go swimming in the most glorious, embracing, gentle ocean of all. For this is within us too, a place that is free of fear, free of limitations, where there are no boundaries, no restrictions!

From the heart we can tame the discursive aspects of the mind by witnessing them as waves on the ocean, by accepting whatever arises and going beyond the limitations. In so doing we reach a different level of experience. No longer locked into the relative world, no longer stuck in the mind believing that this is all there is, we have touched upon something far greater, an experience that is uncluttered, expansive, alive, enriching. Although abstract in its nature, it is just as real as the relative. This is the consciousness of the fifth chakra.

The Fifth Chakra

This chakra is associated with the energy that brings together and unifies the abstract and the relative, it is a bringing of the abstract (and by this we mean the higher, yet deeper and more spiritual qualities) into the relativity of our daily lives. No longer is our practice separate from the rest of our lives, nor is it just something we do. Our lives and our practice become one. Fears and paranoia are removed and we see all things just as they are. For this to happen there is a purification – a letting go of all that which is of a poisonous or unskilful nature and the embracing of that which heals, bringing wholeness and clear awareness. This awakening is gradual, for it is not just a realization but also a learning process in becoming skilful and wise. It is like developing a taste for a rare, fine wine, slowly absorbing the subtle fragrance.

This indicates a shift away from the world of the self and other than self to that which is at one with the truth in all beings. It is the development of the ability to discriminate between what is merely mundane trivia, paranoia or neurosis, and that which is nourishing, uplifting and embracing. As this discrimination awakens, our vision and perception become clear. Then we are able to express the truth in our words as well as our actions. Thus the right speech that we explored earlier becomes a living reality, a natural expression of who we are in our essence.

We have opened ourselves to a level of sensitivity and perception that is deeply meaningful. We can see the different effects skilful or unskilful actions have on ourselves and others, how truthfulness can be so transforming, whle deceit is so limiting. And we see how every thing is intimately connected to all other things. It is not as if we are dismissing the mundane in favour of the abstract, nor are we judging one to be better than the other. Rather there is an interplay of the two and our lives are enriched beyond measure as a result. We begin to experience a different kind of nourishment, a divine nourishment that is like nectar to our being. For truth is the ultimate sweetness.

6

The Wisdom of No-Mind

We have now come to finding that place in ourselves that is non-rational, makes non-sense and is illogical, so that we may discover our no-mind! To find no-mind we have to go out of the mind. As Alan Watts said in *Meditation*,

> To go out of your mind at least once a day is tremendously important. By going out of your mind you come to your senses. If you stay in your mind all the time, you are overrational. In other words, you are like a very rigid bridge which, because it has no give, no craziness in it, is going to be blown down in the first hurricane.

If we do not go out of the mind then, as Watts says, we become judgemental and make things appear as if they are real and solid, we become inflexible, tense, probably stressed and we snap easily. If we break too often then we break down. Breaking down is usually seen as a helpless and hopeless state. But if we can really break down and our props, support systems and limitations are released, then we get a rare glimpse of the irrational madness that lies within us all. Rather than seeing this as conventional madness which has to be put right and made normal again with drugs and psychiatry, perhaps we can see it in its true light – that of crazy wisdom, imbued with irrational sanity!

Moments of such irrationality, of being out of our minds, ultimately keep us sane. However, in moving from the common, everyday state of the ego-centred mind to a state of awakened consciousness we may pass through a phase in which the mind becomes seemingly paranoid, freaked out, deranged or taken apart; it is then rearranged as our experience of reality deepens and we find a new understanding. When disintegration is happening, integration is really taking place. The confusion, depression and suffering experienced as the mind breaks down can actually enable a *breakthrough* to occur, for this is a breaking down of the ego and its attendant illusions. The more we are able to let go of the illusion, the less we suffer. The spiritual teachings are there to help guide us through such a breakdown, so that we do not get lost, discouraged or distracted along the way.

The irrationality of no-mind, of no 'I', lets us see the humour and insubstantiality of life, for if there is no one home then there is no holding on to events and changes, we can bend and play in the wind. Tarthang Tulku, in *Gesture of Balance*, says how,

> Without the 'I' there is no subject, no object, no time. Some people may feel this is insane, but without the 'I' there is no one to go crazy, no demonic influence or person to react to it – only silent awareness. To arrive at this state we simply need to be open . . . When we can remain balanced in the natural state of awareness, then nothing can harm us.

We are not fixed, are not solid. We can move freely, are flexible and spontaneous. We are not static and unable to see beyond our limited views, but rather our vision is everywhere, in all places, able to see the many different facets of any single thing. By being out of the mind we are not tied down to the confines and limited space that being in the mind normally offers.

But what is this mind we are coming out of? Is it just a bundle of desires, of self-created illusions, denials, personalities and memories? Is it this great burden we carry around with us all the time, like a bag of belongings banging the ground behind us? Are we really just antique collectors, storing the many objects in the attics of our minds? And why is it so hard to come out of the mind as we know it and to enter into freedom, to enter into the heart, to radically shift the way we are looking and responding to the world? What is it that stops us from doing this?

The Wisdom of No-Mind

Is it because, in reality, there is no mind? That it is actually a fabricated manifestation that we have created in order to justify our existence? For when there is no ego, what is there? Without ego there is no self, no reference point from which reality comes and goes, nothing to be attached to, no substance or solidity, just emptiness. What is there if there is no-I-thing, nothing to cling to? Is it the fear of this realness, and maybe even the sneaky suspicion that there really is no mind, that stops us from being able to let go? For who are we and what is there when there is no mind?

Form and Emptiness

The fear of emptiness and nothingness and no fixed reference points is a fear that can be replaced with trust. For when we do experience no mind, instead of a fearful emptiness there is actually a complete awareness of now that is totally fulfilling. It is pure beingness. There is no mental chattering filling up the space, so it is certainly empty, yet at the same time it is tremendously rich and full as it is overflowing with *everything*. The very emptiness is pure wisdom and is delightful. There is a beautiful Buddhist stanza that describes this state:

Form is emptiness and the very emptiness is form; emptiness does not differ from form, form does not differ from emptiness; whatever is form, that is emptiness; whatever is emptiness, that is form.

In other words, form has no independent inherent existence. The true nature of form is therefore emptiness; likewise emptiness makes possible the form, as form is established from it, dependent upon circumstances. This is like the banana tree. From the outside the banana tree seems so prolific and bountiful with its great bunches of ripe bananas. Yet if we peel away the trunk of the tree we find that layer after layer of leaves produce only a hollow centre. There is no trunk – in the very middle of the tree is empty space. There is nothing inside. The form is actually empty, there is no-thing, yet the emptiness is also form, there is some-thing, the banana tree.

We are like this. We have such colourful and interesting outsides, all shapes and forms and sizes. Yet if we keep going inside, deeper and deeper, we eventually find emptiness, no form. This image has often concerned the wary ones, for if there is only emptiness then what is the purpose of it all? What are we doing here? And why on earth would we want to discover emptiness? Isn't enlightenment, nirvana, or whatever we call it, supposed to be blissful and the greatest experience possible? What purpose is this if it is just empty? But as Shunryu Suzuki says in *Zen Mind, Beginner's Mind*,

Before we understand the idea of emptiness, everything seems to exist substantially. But after we realize the emptiness of things, everything becomes real – not substantial . . . Thus we realize the true meaning of each tentative existence. When we first hear that everything is a tentative existence, most of us are disappointed; but this . . . is because our way of observing things is so deeply rooted in our self-centred ideas . . . To realize this fact itself is to be relieved of suffering.

The wisdom of no-mind therefore lies in its very emptiness, yet at the same time there is no denying the form that has manifested from it, namely ourselves. And if we have come from emptiness, from the original no-mind and have come into form, then is it not our purpose, our journey, to now return to such emptiness? To rediscover the emptiness within the form? Embarking on such a journey is a heeding to that divine homesickness that calls us, sometimes calling so clearly that we cannot deny it, other times so softly that we have to bend our ear to hear the whispers.

The Journey of the Magi

The story of the three Magi, journeying from their kingdoms in search of the newborn Christ, is rich in symbolism of this spiritual journey leading from delusion to awakening, from the mundane to the divine, from ego to egolessness and no-mind. Father Thomas Keating describes how, 'The Magi are symbols of those who genuinely and painstakingly seek the truth in every generation.' Leaving behind the material lures and sensual delights their kingdoms offered them, these three followed a star, a symbol of universal consciousness, to find its source. And they found it in the lowliest and humblest of abodes, a place free from any form of worldly acclaim. Yet in such a place was brilliant light, a radiance far beyond any that their finest riches had ever offered.

The journey that the Magi undertook was far from easy. It was fraught with disappointments, difficulties and hindrances that only served to make them want to turn back. How they had to battle their desires and discomforts in order to continue, constantly questioning their reason and sanity! As T.S. Eliot describes in his poem, *The Journey of the Magi*,

> There were times we regretted
> The summer palaces on slopes, the terraces,
> And the silken girls bringing sherbet.

This struggle is a known condition of the journey. Not only are there very few who embark, but the lures, distractions and temptations along the way are manifold. It can seem so pointless to continue when everyone around us appears to be having such a good time! Is not ignorance bliss? John White, in *What is Enlightenment?*, talks of this state of conflict experienced on the journey when he says,

> On the spiritual path there are many side trails that are essentially deadends, if not traps. There are also periods of chaotic upheavals

in the mind, moments of insight and partial breakthrough, intervals of exhaustion and utter apathy, and times of intense struggle and doubt when faith in the ultimate importance of the spiritual journey alone carries you stumbling forward.

However, it is the very hardships that make the journey so enriching – through the difficulties we gain greater insight and understanding, there is a stripping away of the superfluous.

The symbolism of there being three Magi, not just one, is vitally important, for there is tremendous and necessary support to be gained from being with fellow travellers. The 'spiritual brotherhood' gives us the knowledge that we are not alone and that we are not completely mad! It is that which supports us through the hard times, enabling us to discern between the worldly lures and the spiritual truths. It also encourages us to continue forward ourselves as we help others through their struggle to reach a state of greater freedom.

In persevering the Magi finally came to their Christ, to discover their own awakening into God consciousness. They found the light of God that they were seeking in a simple place of humility and compassion where no form of hatred or greed existed. There the three rested in the light, experiencing the peace. The stable symbolizes a place free of the material world, a place where all pretensions and fears can be dropped, where there is an embracing of the truth.

Later, in returning to their homelands, the Magi took a different route than the one they had come by, clearly indicating that once we have changed so profoundly within ourselves we can not tread the same path again, can no longer go the way we used to. A new way unfolds – the old has died and there is a birth of the new. The birth that the Magi witnessed, the birth of Christ consciousness, was indeed a birth, yet for it to manifest within us as the birth of Self consciousness it also involves a death – the death of the ego. T.S. Eliot continues in his poem describing the pain involved in such a death,

> Were we led all that way for
> Birth or Death? There was a Birth, certainly,
> We had evidence and no doubt. I had seen birth and
> death,

But had thought they were different; this Birth was
Hard and bitter agony for us, like Death, our
                                                    death.

Normally we associate death with being an end, a finality, that
there is no more. What we are seeing here is how complete
freedom demands the death of our limited self in order for a
true birth to occur. This is the birth of a freedom from illusions, from desire and attachment. It is free because it is not
based on any one thing, it is empty of conditions. It is therefore limitless. Such a birth brings new life, a rejoicing in the
death, for without it such newness could never be experienced.
Thus the poem ends with,

I should be glad of another death.

Letting Go

When we do go beyond the ego and enter into a state of
egolessness, all boundaries dissolve and we become one with
everything. There is no sense of a separate self, of a me-ness
separate to a you-ness, so our experience is not limited to only
that which 'I' experience but is merged into, and therefore is
one with, that which all things experience. The limitations that
keep us locked within a fixed sense of 'this is how I am' are
no longer operative and we become one with everything we
normally think of as being not us.

We become one with and simultaneously experience the
rock, the tree, the sky, the child, the galloping horse, the rain,
the flowers, the wind, the people on a crowded train, the bus
driver and the bus. We are all things and we are no things at
the same time. We do not exist as separate and individual, for
we are one with everything, even though we seemingly do
have a separate existence. This experience is very moving for
nothing else exists in the present moment but awareness,
cognition, present-fullness. No longer bound by mental or
physical realities, we have merged into the universal Self.

The letting go that takes place for this to happen is a letting
go of the fixed idea of how things are or should be. Usually
such letting go is done by going on holiday, getting high or

drunk or being distracted in some other way, so that the details of our lives are temporarily eased. Having a fixed idea of reality serves to keep our fears at bay, to keep us in a safe and secure place where we are not threatened by the unknown. It helps protect us from ourselves. When we are in this fixed state and someone or something threatens our grasp of reality, then it makes our world appear fuzzy or wobbly at the edges, it reveals the insubstantiality of such a fixation.

Generally we will find a way to plug the leak, as it were, so that our boat does not sink. We do this by denying the reality of such a threat, convincing ourselves that we are right and therefore this threat, this unknown, must be wrong. Or we enter into combat, declaring a war on the threat, determined that we are the greater power and will easily overcome such an irritation. Even if our security and image of ourselves is threatened by something undeniable, like the death of a loved one, we will still manage to find ways to explain it so that we can continue without having to confront our relationship to the unknown. Plato said, 'We can easily forgive a child who is afraid of the dark; the real tragedy of life is when men are afraid of the light.'

Truly to let go means having the courage and fearlessness to accept the threat and to open ourselves to whatever effect such acceptance may have on our fixed views. The point is that we can go beyond our suffering and clinging self to what is real. We can, as Lex Hixon says in *The Mother of the Universe*, 'Tame the primal human obsessions – greed, anger, pride, hatred and desire – and use them as powerful bullocks to plow the field of our awareness by day and by night.' If we can see beyond the fear – and we can do this by coming out of the mind, embracing our freedom and living in the heart – then we find that the unknown is not so unknown after all, that the threat is actually imaginary. For freedom is ultimately our most natural state, our divine home, it is the most familar.

The unknown is only unknown while we are living in the past or the future, for living in this way is living in a dream – the past is gone and the future has not happened. However, we drag the past along with us, keeping it alive when it should have died long ago, recalling it and re-living it over and over again, as if trying to find some magic clue to

understanding the present. Or we dream and create all manner
of fantasies of the future, from the wonderful life we shall one
day have, to the deep fear of something going wrong.

When we can live in the present, fully and completely, there
can be no unknown. For there is only now. That doesn't mean
we cannot plan for or consider the future, only that it is done
from a state of awareness of the whole. Instead of drifting
off into daydreams or expending our energy on anxiety and
worry, we are simply at one in the moment. We then find we
have little need for what has gone before, other than as a way
to recognize our repetitive and habitual patterns, to see what
confusion the limited mind can create. To be completely in the
present implies a fearlessness, openness, acceptance, and a
realization that we are not limited by our circumstances.

Alan Watts says,

> The future is a concept – it doesn't exist! There is no such thing as
> tomorrow! There never will be because time is always now.
> That's one of the things we discover when we stop talking to
> ourselves and stop thinking. We find there is only a present, only
> an eternal now.

If we think of time passing it always seems to go either very
quickly or very slowly and we get caught up in excitement or
regret. If we think of just being here and now, where there is no
time, then nothing passes, nothing is ever over, it just is. By
stopping the analysis and evaluation, by accepting things as
they are, there is a quietness. By letting go of how we think
things should be we can experience how things actually are.

Then we see that each and every thing has its own existence.
It is not separate from us, yet nor is it us. Therefore we can let
it be as it is without needing to interfere. We do not have to be
affected by the whims and habits of others, or by events that
take place that we may not like. The irritations and frustra-
tions we might usually feel are replaced by an acceptance of
what is. This need not make us passive but enables us to be in
tune, in the flow of life's unfolding, rather than resisting it. As
Anne Bancroft explains in *The Spiritual Journey*,

> I realized what a lot of time I spent trying to alter the events of the
> day, rather than altering myself. If I accepted burnt toast, for
> instance, as a 'fact', somehow that took away the irritation I

would normally feel and replaced it with a wry admiration of the splendidly black crusts. It did not stop me changing the setting of the toaster but it seemed to make the whole situation easy instead of heavy.

In China this is seen as being in the Tao. As we allow each thing to assume its natural place, where we do not have to be in charge, there is a remarkable freedom that pours in and through us. We become like the surfer riding with the waves, or the dancer feeling the rhythm of the music in perfect harmony.

Letting go implies there is no imposition of ourselves and thus we are both completely I-less, yet simultaneously in relationship with every thing. Then our actions are genuine, for our decisions are not distorted by prejudice. It is a releasing of attachment. If we are attached then we impose ourselves in some way and influence the situation by projecting our impressions on to it. Any relationship we have is therefore an illusion, for it is actually a relationship with our projections rather than with the thing itself.

Normally we do not relate to the rain, for instance, as simply rain, but are relating to our ideas and feelings about rain. Those feelings we are projecting outwards influence our experience of rain, making it either pleasurable or burdensome: 'Oh no, it's going to ruin my day', or 'How wonderful as the earth is so dry.' If we have no projections and see there is just rain – neither good nor bad – then there are no judgements, it simply is, complete and exactly as it is meant to be. We realize we are not the doers but rather the witnesses.

From self to Self

There are different beliefs concerning the way to deal with the ego and to becoming egoless – a lively and spontaneous state, where we are not identified with the self. Some say the ego must be annihilated, while others say it dissolves as we reach higher states of awareness. These different approaches have often been misunderstood as the idea of annihilation can give rise to guilt – that it is wrong to relate through the ego, that it must be gone – while the idea of natural dissolution can give rise to lethargy, to a lack of effort.

There is no doubt that our sense of self is very real and valid, we do have feelings, sensations, an 'I' that does things, that learns, thinks and creates. And there are times when the ego serves an important function in our growth, pushing us towards a greater happiness, generating a desire for more knowledge and less warring. The ego can actually be the very seed of our awakening. As Khentin Tai Situpa says in *Way To Go*,

> We know what we want and what we do not want. We know when we are happy and unhappy; thus we can understand how others can feel happy or unhappy. We can understand their suffering. Applying how 'I' feel to others can give birth to compassion.

Rather than denying or annihilating either our selves or the ego, what we can do is go beyond the limitations and the hold of the fixed idea of self – the illusion of self that causes so much fear, pain and confusion – to see that this 'I' exists only on the relative level. The 'I' is a relative truth, but on the absolute level no independent 'I' exists. Then there is a complete surrender, a merging and oneness with God consciousness.

So it is not as if there is no self. It is simply that this is only a part of the picture and we are rarely aware of the rest of the landscape. There is a relative, real and valid self, one that has feelings and thoughts and impressions. And there is an absolute Self that is not separate to the relative, yet does not identify with it. For the absolute Self is in all and is one with all. Dzigar Kongtrul Rinpoche says,

> The gross mind is called relative. The subtle mind is called absolute. The mind is gross in that it is not the truth. It does not see the truth. This 'self' we create, our life and daily routines, are relative in that they change. Anything that changes cannot be true because the truth never changes. When we have some intellectual understanding of that, then we can have some experience of seeing the absolute mind.

One of the most significant ways in which we limit ourselves and maintain our relativity is by believing that our idea of self is going to go on for ever. This is not necessarily voiced as a fear of death, although that can certainly be one expression, but rather as a complete inability to conceive of there even being no 'I'. We prefer to hold on to and believe that we are, in some way, permanent. This belief that we are permanent or solid is the major cause of our separation from each other. It fuels our fears of being attacked, keeping us in a state of hostility and self-protection. How can we merge and be at one with everything if this 'I' is a separate and sustaining entity? It immediately creates boundaries, and boundaries have to be maintained and protected.

Recognizing the impermanence of *all* things, let alone the self, means we no longer view life in quite the same way. For impermanence is the underlying factor that unifies and pervades everything. The integration of such a recognition completely shifts our perspective. We find there is a transparency to life, we can see through things and this gives a ridiculous-like quality to our behaviour! The struggle to protect and preserve ourselves becomes like a child's game; we see how we are constantly trying to manipulate and dominate events so as to avoid confronting the nakedness of our impermanence. This can only make us laugh at our own actions! Believing we are fixed means we can easily be broken, becoming transparent means there is nothing to break.

The Six Perfections

The realization of this understanding needs to be integrated and to have a means of expression. Recognizing truth is not enough – there also has to be integration so that our lives actually change. For how do we behave in the world as awakened beings? How do we put into practice that which is now more meaningful to us than anything else could possibly be?

To help us there are what are known as the six perfections, although the word *perfection* can actually be translated from the original Sanskrit word *paramita* more clearly as meaning 'that which will carry us to the other shore'. The paramitas therefore offer us a guideline we can steer by as we make our crossing.

First Perfection: Generosity

The first perfection is that of generosity. This does not mean that we should go around giving to all who are in need regardless, for giving in this way is not always appropriate. Rather we give what is worthwhile, what is skilful and will genuinely help another person. Most importantly we give it freely, without attachment, for if we have attachment to our giving then it is not a giving but a wanting. True generosity implies that our motivation be clear and not tainted by ego desires, by wanting to get something in return, or from a fear of appearing selfish. To give in a skilful way does not mean we have to give materially – even if we own nothing we can give with a smile, with a caring thought, with our hearts.

Being generous also means being willing to let go of our fears and habitual patterns, for holding on to these creates pain and suffering for others – it is not pleasant to see another person suffering – so this is a selfish act. By letting go of our own limitations and neuroses we are giving to others in a very generous and caring way. When we are being selfish we are thinking only of ourselves, so how can we also be thinking of others or of God? When we are selfless then we can give to all beings and be one with God.

When we give truly and without desire for return, then it is extraordinary how the universe will give back to us. We knew a nun who suffered very badly from the cold so she always wore a warm scarf wrapped around her neck. One year, at Christmas, all the members in her monastery were asked to give something that was meaningful to them so that the poorer and more needy people of the local community could receive gifts. This particular nun chose to give her scarf, for she was well aware of her attachment to it. A month later she went on tour to teach in different cities around the country. When she arrived at her first teaching engagement she found, lying on her bed, a beautiful mohair scarf, with an explanation from her host that he hoped it would help keep her warm in the chilly evenings. By the end of that tour, the nun had received four different scarves!

Second Perfection: Skilful Conduct

This implies being able to refrain from any action that causes pain or harm to another, as well as that which is selfish or has a misguided motivation. It also means practising that which is positive, in particular a spiritual discipline or faith which helps further develop our awareness and sensitivity. Skilful conduct also includes actions that are for the benefit of others even if they are unaware of such actions. If we need acknowledgement for what we do, then are these actions truly unconditional? The motivating factor in our conduct should be to do whatever we can to enable others to find the truth within themselves.

Third Perfection: Forbearance

This is especially important as it brings any ego-centred attachments we may have straight to the surface! Forbearance is the ability to 'bear before'; it means being able to refrain from hurting someone even if they have hurt us – not having to retaliate despite the incitement. If someone hits us and we strike them back, then they have really had an effect on us, their blow has gone far deeper than the flesh; if we do not strike back then their blow falls short of their mark and we remain at peace. This is realizing that we cannot fight fire with fire. It does not mean we should be like doormats to be walked over, but with insight we can be skilful in dealing with each situation.

Forbearance also implies being able to cope with whatever pain we have in our lives. We don't have to look for pain or suffering, there is more than enough without that! But we do not have to fight it, resist it, or resent others for making it happen. This is especially the case when our pain is due to someone else's actions – how easy it is to feel bitter and to want justice. But this simply increases the suffering even more for everyone involved. When we can surrender to the situation with forbearance then the suffering is free to go and is replaced with compassion. Being mindful in these situations is the key to understanding for then we can see through the suffering and it is easier to bear.

Fourth Perfection: Diligence

Like a coat of armour that protects us from assault or weapons, so diligence protects us from laziness and doubt, the hindrances that so easily distract. Here we apply energy and commitment to all of our actions, the commitment to be at one with the truth. We determine not to be deterred or led off course, but are diligent in our effort to stay focused. We are also diligent in our desire to learn, to be open and receptive to whatever can help ourselves or others. The Buddha stated very clearly that we should not accept his teachings without first questioning them and seeing if they are appropriate for our own lives. In this way we do not become dependent and conditioned by another's teachings or methods but are able to find a level of truth that is right for each one of us. This is the beginner's mind – without structure, yet bright and focused.

Fifth Perfection: Meditation

As we have discussed previously, meditation is the development of an inner awareness that enables us to see the mind for what it really is, beneath the constant chatter and neurosis. From this awareness arises calmness and clarity and the genuine, heartfelt desire to help all sentient beings. Meditation provides a space, a rest from our endless search for happiness. In this space we can be healed. Heaven is a space of eternal rest, it is that state of love that rests even in the midst of action.

Sixth Perfection: Wisdom

This is the wisdom that takes us from seeing the relative skilful and unskilful effects of our actions, to the awareness of complete non-duality, where the concepts of skilful and unskilful do not even exist. Applying this wisdom means that our lives are imbued with the truth, our every action, thought, word and emotion are expressions of such truth.

Sixth and Seventh Chakras

This brings us to the highest levels of consciousness and of awakening – the awareness of God consciousness – and that of the sixth and seventh chakras. The consciousness of the sixth chakra is the realization of our inner vision. It is also known as The Third Eye, as here the eye of wisdom focuses on the transcendent wisdom within, rather than on the illusionary wisdom of the world. We are merging with the knowledge of awakened mind and it manifests as our ability to perceive reality with absolute clarity. The consciousness of the sixth chakra is where we enter into God consciousness, there is the pure light of truth and we transcend worldly awareness. It is the realization of our God nature.

In experiencing the consciousness of the sixth chakra we see the world as non-dual, there is a relief in the awakening to God consciousness as the substratum of all existence. The traps and discursive games of the mind become clear; how we solidify the ego; we realize the connectedness of all things; and we see how we are therefore no one thing. The ego is redundant, it has no ground, we are in a state of surrender so the true Self emerges, brilliant and joyous. It is as if we were driving in the fog and cannot see when suddenly we put our headlamps on and the road becomes clear ahead of us. There is no more illusion or deception. However, we have yet to experience final awakening where the ego dissolves entirely by merging into the absolute.

The consciousness of the seventh chakra is our full awakening, the father and son are one, God consciousness is all there is. Before the seventh chakra awareness we have glimpses of reality of truth. Now we are in living grace, we merge into the cosmic ocean. The consciousness of the sixth chakra sees the light of realization but there is still an awareness of self and other than self, even though there is also the awareness that there is no difference between the two. Now even the awareness of two dissolves.

This is the end of individual existence, the end of suffering, the final surrender into absolute oneness and pure bliss. This state has been called Nirvana, Nirvikalpa Samadhi, Enlightenment, God consciousness, or Divine Communion. It is the fulfilment of our purpose for being here, the answer to all the questions, the freeing of man from the bounds of limitation. Now our purpose in life is purely for the benefit of all sentient beings. We are free of ignorance, the veil of illusion, we see God in all things and live for that truth.

Each of us may have our own understanding and expression of the enlightened state, ranging from an experience of the higher Self to the image of a figure bathed in light. However we may define this, one thing is certain. Enlightenment or God is invisible. It cannot be categorized, seen with our two eyes, analyzed, or labelled. In other words God, or God consciousness is in-visible, actually meaning it is visible with the inner eye of awareness. Therefore we are God, just as a drop of water is one with the rain that falls, with the water in the pool, with the river that flows into the ocean, and with the ocean itself. God consciousness is our true nature, the essence of all life.

As long as we project God outside of ourselves, or see God as something never attainable, then we shall remain in a state of duality. When we open our hearts and purify our minds through surrender then we can find the beauty of the Self within. Then we know we are not different from the truth. This is the true guru – the inner voice of insight, the glory and joy of being alive, the freedom from all delusions. This joy, this peace, is not something we get for then it could be something we can lose. Rather it is inherent at all times. But we are like the musk deer that has a wonderful scent in its belly yet roams the country searching for this scent! So we search everywhere for answers, for truth, not realizing that we have it with us always, that we are it.

There are many different ways of expressing the awakened state, depending upon our view, for the various traditional religious and spiritual paths have constantly exposed this truth. The place where these expressions meet, like the spokes of a wheel converging at the hub, is in recognizing that truth is inherent within each and every one of us, equally, no matter who or what we may be. To follow one path is to recognize the truth in all paths.

The Quakers talk of 'Walking over the surface of the earth meeting that of God in every man', while the Buddha said that Buddha-nature, the essence of the enlightened mind, is inherent in all life; it has only to be recognized. Hence we find stories of murderers or criminals who, seeing the futility and destructive nature of their actions, become freed from their limited mind-set and discover their true Self. Jesus urged us to awaken and to repent, not so much for our sins as for our loss of God consciousness. The Greek interpretation of the word repent is *metanoia*, literally meaning to go beyond or higher than the ordinary mental state. To repent is therefore to transform our ego-centred self into that which is one with God. In this way we awaken to our true Self and can enter the kingdom of God, we are healed of our alienation and become whole.

The world's religions and faiths also meet in their recognition of the illusion of separation, that we are not isolated beings wandering in our own worlds. The awareness of our connectedness and inter-relatedness, how we are all intricately linked together is described by Joanna Macy in *Despair and Personal Power in the Nuclear Age*,

> From Judaism, Christianity and Islam to Hinduism, Buddhism, Taoism and Native American and Goddess religions, each offers images of the sacred web into which we are woven. We are called children of one God and 'members of one body'; we are seen as drops in the ocean of Brahman; we are pictured as jewels in the Net of Indra. We interexist – like synapses in the mind of an all-encompassing being.

What is Enlightenment?

We have still to ask the question: what is Samadhi, Enlightenment, God consciousness? Is it even explainable? Is it beyond words and definition?

In the Buddhist tradition, enlightenment is seen as a state where there is no state to be – just clear awareness of things as they are, that which transcends the duality of subject and object. This is transcendental wisdom, free from all concepts. Enlightenment is also understood as pure being-ness, thus the most profound and deepest state of compassion, an overflowing of unconditional love equally towards all sentient beings. This compassion is expressed in the total desire that all beings be freed from suffering and realize their true Self. These two aspects – wisdom and compassion – are like the two sides of the same coin, or the two hands that spring from the same body. The awakening of these two qualities enables full enlightenment to be realized.

However, this description can sound somewhat grandiose and it is important to remember that awakening to our true nature is real and possible for each one of us. Lex Hixon writes in *What is Enlightenment?*

Enlightenment is not an isolated attainment of ancient or legendary sages but a process flowering through members of every culture, a process in which our consciousness gradually becomes transparent to its own intrinsic nature.

We are always and constantly in the process of being enlightened. It is not a fixed state that at some point we attain. Nor is it only for the chosen few. For enlightenment is nothing more than the merging with what we already are in essence, a constantly changing, opening and expanding state. It is a letting go of all that is not. This is our natural heritage and is totally ordinary. All the limitations we impose on to this state are the extra-ordinary ones.

As enlightenment is our true Self, so it is not a gaining of anything or the attainment of something special; it is not the development of psychic or paranormal powers; nor is it something that takes us off to some far celestial realm; it is not even an altered state of consciousness. As Ken Wilber says in *What is Enlightenment?*, 'The Ultimate state of Consciousness . . . is known not one among many but one without a second . . . it is not an altered state of consciousness for there is no alternative to it.'

Enlightenment is simply the manifestation of being, that which is always becoming, that which is what we always have been and always will be. Ramana Maharshi explains in *The Spiritual Teachings of Ramana Maharshi*,

> There is no reaching the Self. If the Self were to be reached, it would mean that the Self is not here and now but is yet to be obtained. What is got afresh will also be lost. So it will be impermanent. What is not permanent is not worth striving for. So I say that the Self is not reached. You are the Self; you are already That.

If enlightenment – the experience of no-mind – is who we really are, then is it not our purpose for being here to come to this understanding? Or, as Fritz Pearls said, to lose our minds and come to our senses. And if so, then when will we do it? For as Echu, the Zen poet, wrote,

> It is a rare privilege
> to be born as a human being, as
> we happen to be;
> If we do not achieve enlightenment in this life,
> when do we expect to achieve it?

Bibliography

Bancroft, Anne, *The Spiritual Journey*, Element Books, Shaftesbury, Dorset, 1991.

Bly, Robert, *Iron John*, Element Books, Shaftesbury, Dorset, 1991.

Chodron, Pema, *The Wisdom of No Escape and The Path of Loving Kindness*, Shambhala, Boston, Massachusetts, 1991.

Dalai Lama, His Holiness, *Kindness, Clarity and Insight*, Snow Lion Publications, Ithaca, New York, 1984.

Dzigar Kontrol, Rinpoche,` The Depths of Your Mind`, Nexus Magazine, Boulder, Colorado, November, 1990.

Eliot, T.S., *The Waste Land and other Poems*, A Harvest/HBJ Book, New York, 1962.

Ferguson, Marilyn, *The Aquarian Conspiracy*, Jeremy P. Tarcher, Los Angeles, California, 1980.

Hixon, Lex, *The Mother of the Universe*, unpublished essay.
What is Enlightenment?, ed. John White, Jeremy P. Tarcher, Los Angeles, California, 1984.

Keating, Father Thomas, *The Way Ahead*, ed. Eddie and Debbie Shapiro, Element Books, Shaftesbury, Dorset, 1992.

Krishna, Gopi, *What is Enlightenment?*, ed. John White, Jeremy P. Tarcher, Los Angeles, California, 1984.

Macy, Joanna, *Despair and Power in the Nuclear Age*, New Society Publishers, Philadelphia, 1983.

Maharshi, Ramana, *The Spiritual Teachings of Ramana Maharshi*, Shambhala, Boston, Massachusetts, 1988.

Merton, Thomas, *The New Man*, Farrar, Straus & Giroux, New York, 1961.

Nhat Hanh, Thich, *Every Breath You Take*, The New Age Journal, Los Angeles, California, November, 1990.
A Guide To Walking Meditation, A Fellowship Book, Nyack, New York, 1985.

Norbu, Namkhai, *The Cycle of Day and Night*, Station Hill Press, Barrytown, New York, 1987.

Sangharakshita, *Human Enlightenment*, Windhorse Publications, Glasgow, 1980.

Shapiro, Debbie, *The Bodymind Workbook*, Element Books, Shaftesbury, Dorset, 1990.

Shapiro, Eddie, *Inner Conscious Relaxation*, Element Books, Shaftesbury, Dorset, 1990.

Smith, Huston, *The Religions of Man*, Harper & Row, New York, 1958.

Suzuki, Shunryu, *Zen Mind, Beginner's Mind*, Weatherhill, New York, 1970.

Tai Situpa, Khentin, *Way To Go*, Kagyu Samye Ling, Langholm, Dumfriesshire, 1985.

Tarthang, Tulku, *Gesture of Balance*, Dharma Publishing, California, 1977.

Trungpa, Chogyum, *The Myth of Freedom*, Shambhala, Boston, Massachusetts, 1976.

Shambhala: The Sacred Path of the Warrior, Shambhala, Boston, Massachusetts, 1984.

Watts, Alan, *Meditation*, Celestial Arts, Millbrae, California, 1974.

White, John, *What is Enlightenment?*, Jeremy P. Tarcher, Los Angeles, California, 1984.

Wilbur, Ken, *What is Enlightenment?*, ed. John White, Jeremy P. Tarcher, Los Angeles, California, 1984.

Index